The ITSM Process Design Guide

Developing, Reengineering, and
Improving IT Service Management

Donna Knapp, CPDE, ITIL Expert™

Copyright ©2010 ITSM Academy

ISBN-13: 978-1-60427-049-5

Printed and bound in the U.S.A. Printed on acid-free paper.

10 9 8 7 6 5 4 3 2 1

Library of Congress Cataloging-in-Publication Data

Knapp, Donna.
  The ITSM process design guide : developing, reengineering, and improving
IT service management / by Donna Knapp.
    p. cm.
  Includes bibliographical references and index.
  ISBN 978-1-60427-049-5 (hardcover : alk. paper)
    1. Information technology—Management. 2. Information technology—Quality
control. 3. Information resources management. 4. Organizational change.
I. Title.
  HD30.2.K6293 2010
  004.068—dc22
                            2010019183

  This publication contains information obtained from authentic and highly regarded sources. Re-
printed material is used with permission, and sources are indicated. Reasonable effort has been made
to publish reliable data and information, but the author and the publisher cannot assume responsibility for the validity of all materials or for the consequences of their use.
  All rights reserved. Neither this publication nor any part thereof may be reproduced, stored in a
retrieval system, or transmitted in any form or by any means, electronic, mechanical, photocopying,
recording or otherwise, without the prior written permission of the publisher.
  The copyright owner's consent does not extend to copying for general distribution for promotion,
for creating new works, or for resale. Specific permission must be obtained from J. Ross Publishing
for such purposes.
  Direct all inquiries to J. Ross Publishing, Inc., 5765 N. Andrews Way, Fort Lauderdale, FL 33309.

Phone: (954) 727-9333
Fax: (561) 892-0700
Web: www.jrosspub.com

Contents

The following acronymns are used throughout this text.	
Acronym	**Definition**
BPM	Business Process Management
BPR	Business Process Reengineering
CMMI	Capability Maturity Model® Integration
COBIT	Control Objectives for Information and related Technology
CPDE	Certified Process Design Engineer
CSF	Critical Success Factor
DMADV	Six Sigma—Define, Measure, Analyze, Design, Verify
DMAIC	Six Sigma—Define, Measure, Analyze, Improve, Control
ISG	IT Steering Group
ITUP	IBM Tivoli Unified Process
ITIL®	Information Technology Infrastructure Library®
ITSM	IT Service Management
ISO	International Organization for Standardization
KPI	Key Performance Indicator
MOF	Microsoft® Operations Framework
OCM	Organizational Change Management
OLA	Operational Level Agreement
PDCA	Plan, Do, Check, Act
PDD	Process Definition Document
PIT	Process Improvement Team
PMF	ITIL® Process Maturity Framework
PMO	Project Management Office
QMS	Quality Management System
RACI	Responsible, Accountable, Consulted, Informed
RACIVS	Responsible, Accountable, Consulted, Informed, Verifies, Signs off

The following acronymns are used throughout this text.	
Acronym	**Definition**
RASCI	Responsible, Accountable, Supports, Consulted, Informed
RDD	Requirements Definition Document
RFI	Request for Information
RFP	Request for Proposal
ROI	Return on Investment
SLA	Service Level Agreement
SLM	Service Level Management
SLR	Service Level Requirement
PMBOK	Project Management Body of Knowledge
PRINCE2	Projects in Controlled Environments
SMART	Specific, Measurable, Achievable, Realistic, and Timely
TQC	Total Quality Control

Preface

"Where do we begin?" "How do we keep the momentum going?" I can't tell how many times I've been asked these questions. There is a wealth of best practice guidance available to organizations looking to design and improve IT service management (ITSM) processes, but what's often missing are the step-by-step methods and techniques. This book is designed to provide that "how to" guide.

I understand how challenging it is for organizations to undertake process design and improvement initiatives while at the same time, "holding down the fort." I've experienced the difficulties that accompany changing an organization's culture and I have seen how technology can both help and become a hindrance. I also know that many of you have been asked to adopt complex frameworks and standards with inadequate training, tools, and information. The goal of this book is to provide the practical guidance and insight you need to overcome these challenges. Whether your organization is looking to design a single process, undertake a comprehensive ITSM program, or integrate multiple frameworks and standards, this book is dedicated to helping you succeed.

Individuals new to process design will find a proven roadmap that describes where to begin, what to do, and how to do it. Seasoned professionals will find an easy to use reference guide that is packed with checklists, "how to" techniques, and sample deliverables such as documents, plans, and templates. All readers will appreciate this guide's easy to read style and holistic approach to process design and improvement.

The Intended Audience

This book is intended for readers who:

- Require a deep understanding of ITSM process assessment, design, implementation, integration, and management techniques.

- Work in an organization that has adopted one or more ITSM or quality management frameworks or standards and want to understand how to use them as part of a continual improvement program.
- Are leading or participating in process design and improvement initiatives. Relevant roles include IT professionals, process owners, process managers, process champions, process stakeholders, and project managers.
- Wish to enhance their role-based capabilities in activities such as defining and analyzing customer requirements, assessing process maturity, producing meaningful metrics, managing organizational change, or selecting process-enabling technologies.
- Have a project management background and want to understand process design and management techniques.
- Wish to become a Certified Process Design Engineer (CPDE)®

Certified Process Design Engineer (CPDE)®

Introduced by Loyalist Certification Services (LCS) in June of 2008, the Certified Process Design Engineer (CPDE)® certification is designed to impart, test, and validate knowledge on best practices in the assessment, design, implementation, integration, and management of ITSM processes. This book serves as the definitive reference guide for the CPDE certification and so can be used by accredited training organizations to prepare course materials or by individuals to prepare for the exam. The CPDE certification recognizes the important role that a skilled process design engineer plays within an organization.

The CPDE certification has been endorsed as complementary to the IT Infrastructure Library® (ITIL®) Version 3 Qualification Scheme by APM Group, the official accreditor of the OGC ITIL portfolio. The CPDE qualification has been awarded a credit value of 1.5, which can be used by candidates who successfully achieve the certification towards the ITIL Expert™ level of certification. Additional information can be found at: www.itil-officialsite.com/Qualifications/Comple mentaryQualifications.asp.

Approach

This book provides a holistic look at the activities involved in designing and improving ITSM processes. The book begins with a discussion about the changing role of IT and the importance of ITSM processes. The benefits of using existing process frameworks and standards are discussed and the most commonly used ITSM frameworks and standards are described.

Using a project-like approach, chapters are dedicated to topics such as defining and analyzing customer requirements, selecting a process design approach, defining and documenting processes, assessing the maturity of existing processes, designing or redesigning processes, and using proven tools and techniques and meaningful metrics to continually improve your processes. Each of these chapters provide proven step-by-step methods and techniques you can implement immediately whether you are developing a process from scratch, radically redesigning or reengineering a process, or striving to fine-tune a process in an effort to increase its return on investment. As it is a great challenge, an entire chapter is devoted to managing organizational and culture change. A chapter also describes how to evaluate and select process-enabling technologies, once process design activities are complete.

Although this book is very "how to" oriented, it also describes the bigger picture benefits of using proven techniques and existing frameworks and standards to design and improve processes. To derive maximum benefit from this book, you can choose to be an active participant in the learning process. The end-of-chapter discussion topics encourage you to expand your knowledge by discussing the concepts with others. Review questions are designed to reinforce your understanding of key concepts.

Assumed Knowledge

This book assumes that are you familiar with the following topics, either through course work, work experience, or life experience:

* Basic ITSM concepts
* The context of process assessment, design, implementation, integration, and management within a business environment
* Exposure to or experience working with one or more ITSM or quality management frameworks or standards such as:
  ○ Information Technology Infrastructure Library® (ITIL®)
  ○ Control Objectives for Information and related Technology (COBIT®)
  ○ Microsoft® Operations Framework (MOF)
  ○ ISO/IEC 20000
  ○ Total Quality Management (TQM)
  ○ The Malcolm Baldrige National Quality Award
  ○ Capability Maturity Model® Integration (CMMI)
  ○ Six Sigma and Lean Six Sigma
  ○ ISO 9000 and ISO 9001

Overview

This book takes a detailed looked at all aspects of process design and improvement. Each chapter explores a topic, method or technique that contributes to an overall understanding of how to effectively develop, reengineer, or improve ITSM processes.

Chapter 1, Introduction, describes the benefits of efficient and effective ITSM processes and introduces four critical components that must be considered to achieve those benefits. The changing role of IT is discussed in the context of business process management (BPM). The importance of ITSM processes is discussed along with the benefits of using existing frameworks and standards to both develop processes and assess their maturity.

Chapter 2, Defining and Analyzing Customer Requirements, describes formal techniques that can be used to determine customer requirements. How to categorize and translate those requirements into opportunities and options for improvement is described, along with how to prioritize those opportunities.

Chapter 3, Quality Management Principles, describes quality-related frameworks and standards that organizations can use to drive process design and improvement activities. Process design considerations that are discussed include prioritizing process design initiatives and selecting a process design approach.

Chapter 4, Defining and Documenting Processes, describes the six key components of a process and introduces a key deliverable—the process definition document. This chapter also defines the role of policies, processes, procedures, plans, projects, and programs in a top-down approach to process design.

Chapter 5, Assessing Process Maturity, describes how to assess the current level of process maturity as an important part of continual process improvement. The characteristics and challenges of each stage of maturity are described, along with transition steps for moving to the next level of maturity.

Chapter 6, Process Design and Improvement Steps, introduces a ten-step methodology for designing and improving processes, regardless of maturity level. This methodology provides the common vocabulary, tools, and techniques needed to engage process stakeholders.

Chapter 7, Process Design and Improvement Tools and Techniques, introduces proven tools and techniques that can be used to document, design, and continually improve processes such as process maps, the seven basic tools of quality, business cases, return on investment (ROI) calculations, and RACI matrices.

Chapter 8, Producing Meaningful Metrics, describes how to use metrics to control, measure, predict, and improve process performance. This chapter describes the characteristics of meaningful metrics and includes a ten-step approach to implementing a metrics program.

Chapter 9, Managing Organizational Change, describes why organizational change management is a critical success factor when implementing new and improved processes. A five-step program describes how to prepare, motivate, and equip people to meet new business challenges.

Features

To aid you in fully understanding ITSM process design and improvement concepts, the following features in this book are designed to improve its pedagogical value:

- **Figures and tables:** Figures help you visualize important concepts. Tables list conceptual items and examples in a visual and readable format.
- **Quick tips:** Short tips provide practical advice and proven strategies related to the concept being discussed.
- **Definitions:** Boldfaced terms are defined in the glossary of terms.
- **Chapter summaries:** Each chapter is followed by a concise summary of the chapter's concepts. These summaries provide a helpful way to recap and revisit the ideas covered in each chapter.
- **Discussion topics and review questions:** End-of-chapter activities include topics designed to encourage discussion and debate, along with a set of review questions that reinforce the main ideas introduced in each chapter.

Acknowledgments

Publishing a book is a team effort and each and every person's contribution is valued and appreciated. I'd like to first thank the industry professionals and educators who reviewed the draft manuscript, made suggestions, and contributed content that significantly enhanced the quality and completeness of this book. Valued contributors and team mates at ITSM Academy include Jayne Groll, Lisa Schwartz, Michael Cardinal, and Gerri Sasso. Joyce Parker, instructor extraordinaire, has graciously reviewed every book that I've ever written and also contributed content to this book.

Special thanks to Chantell Smith for being such a tremendous advocate for this material. Great thanks also to Julia Chapelle and the entire team at Loyalist Certification Services, as well as APM Group and the members of the ITIL® Qualification Board, for recognizing the value of this material and for endorsing the Certified Process Design Engineer (CPDE)® qualification as complementary to the ITIL Version 3 qualifications scheme.

Thank you to everyone at J. Ross Publishing who contributed their talents to the creation of this book including Steve Buda, VP of New Business Development, and all the people who work "behind the scenes."

As always, love and thanks to my family for your support and encouragement.

And finally, thank you to the many clients and students I have had the privilege to work with during my career. I have learned a great deal from each of you and I bring all of that experience to this book.

Donna Knapp
Tampa, Florida

About the Author

Donna Knapp has over twenty five years experience in the IT industry working as a practitioner, consultant, and trainer. She is a currently working with ITSM Academy as Curriculum Development Manager. Donna holds the ITIL® Service Manager and ITIL® Expert™ certifications, and is a member of the ITIL® V3 International Examination Panel. She holds the ISO/IEC 20000 Foundation and Consultants certifications and is a Certified Process Design Engineer (CPDE)®.

Donna is the author of two college textbooks, *A Guide to Service Desk Concepts, Third Edition* and *A Guide to Customer Service Skills for Service Desk Professionals, Third Edition*. She has developed a number of highly successful seminars including: "Achieving Customer Service Excellence for Service Desk Professionals" and "Building a Service Desk Using ITIL® Best Practices."

Prior to joining ITSM Academy, Donna spent fifteen years working as an independent consultant and trainer in IT service management and help desk/service desk management. She has successfully assisted a wide variety of customers with the design and implementation of IT service management processes and tools.

Donna's client list is impressive and includes engagements at companies such as Coca-Cola Enterprises, CompuCom Systems, National Association of Securities Dealers (NASDAQ), and NCR Corporation. Her experience includes determining requirements and helping clients to evaluate and choose automated IT service management tools, defining key processes such as incident, problem, change, request, configuration, and service level management, and managing the associated implementation efforts.

Donna is known as an innovative provider of consulting, mentoring, and training services and she is frequently asked to speak on issues surrounding IT service management and the service desk. Her personal objective is to creatively promote the processes and technologies required to provide superior customer and technical support and to remain dedicated to life-long learning. She brings to every engagement her practical experience and knowledge of IT service management topics from design to implementation to on-going management.

Foreword

This book represents more than a labor of love; it is a true commitment to growing and learning. For as long as I have known her, Donna Knapp has been actively involved in improving and ensuring the growth of the IT service management community. Donna's dedication to learning and teaching others sets an example for all of her readers. She inspires all of us to reach beyond our normal capacities.

The evolution of this book began as many new ideas do; a group of respected colleagues acknowledging that the enclosed information would provide the learning community with a unique opportunity. Achieving greater efficiency and effectiveness by using proven IT service management best practice frameworks and standards, and proven step-by-step methods and techniques, to design and improve their processes.

The Value Chain

Donna Knapp recognized that the service management audience had access to several best practice frameworks and standards, but no book or course existed to transition the theory to practice. Donna is uniquely positioned to provide this service. Her journey through the service management community as a practitioner, consultant, and trainer provides her with many of the insights needed to deliver a quality product. Donna embarked on the creation of this book and along the way, sought feedback from a team of reviewers with comparable "been there, done that" experience.

Thanks to that expertise, you will have many "aha" moments as you learn proven methods and techniques for customizing and integrating IT service management best practices within your work culture.

The Author

Donna Knapp's talent is evident as you migrate through this book. Her ability to communicate is refined and enhanced by her combined knowledge of theory and practice. As the theory aspect of this book demands, she holds multiple IT service management certifications including those related to ISO/IEC 20000 and Microsoft® Operations Framework. She is an ITIL® Service Manager and was one of the first candidates globally to achieve the ITIL Expert™ certification. She also has spent over 25 years in the IT industry putting that theory into practice.

Industry Trends

One of the things I value most about this book is the current information provided about the IT sector and its quest to use best practice processes. The illumination of trends in this marketplace helps information technology professionals see that they are not the only ones struggling with this journey. Challenges are discussed with great insight and then the value add is that you are provided with actual methods to support and guide you through designing and improving these processes. The recognized cultural shifts discussed in this book will resonate with anyone who has participated in the IT industry for the last decade.

> *This book provides a step-by-step approach to creating and using processes to increase the efficiency and effectiveness of your IT organization.*

Answers delivered in this book include how to reach your customers effectively and how to measure their responses. For example, in our business as an examination institute we are currently using a customer relationship management (CRM) system and a customized database solution. My requirement is to conduct a needs analysis to ensure that we are using both tools efficiently. This book provides me with a methodology for conducting a needs analysis.

This book provokes the reader out of isolation into a forum that provides not just the *why* of using best practices to design and improve their processes, but also the *how*. As best practice frameworks and standards continue to grow in popularity, this requirement is not going to change. Information technology leaders will continue to be expected to come to the table leading the discussion on how IT services and their supporting processes can improve business practices.

Conclusion

> *At the end of this book, readers are able to lead*
> *an effective, measurable, and integrated process*
> *improvement program within their organization.*

The existence of this book is really a testimonial to the entrepreneurial talent of the authoring team and their focus and understanding from a practitioner's perspective of what was missing in the marketplace.

As a partner on this project—Loyalist is the accrediting body for the Certified Process Design Engineer (CPDE)® certification for which this book is the definitive source—it is wonderful to see Donna's effort result in such a well-written, useful book. Good luck on your continued journey of learning and congratulations to Donna for supporting all of us in this quest!

Julia Chapelle
Director
Loyalist Certification Services

Web
Added
Value™

Free value-added materials available from
*the Download Resource Center at **www.jrosspub.com***

At J. Ross Publishing we are committed to providing today's professional with practical, hands-on tools that enhance the learning experience and give readers an opportunity to apply what they have learned. That is why we offer free ancillary materials available for download on this book and all participating Web Added Value™ publications. These online resources may include interactive versions of material that appears in the book or supplemental templates, worksheets, models, plans, case studies, proposals, spreadsheets, and assessment tools, among other things. Whenever you see the WAV™ symbol in any of our publications, it means bonus materials accompany the book and are available from the Web Added Value™ Download Resource Center at www.jrosspub.com.

Downloads for *The ITSM Process Design Guide* include templates, plans, and checklists such as a sample process definition document, document control sheet, high-level implementation plan, key performance indicator checklist, and communication and training plans.

1

Introduction

In today's competitive business climate it's not enough to do things right; Information Technology (IT) organizations must do the right things right. The purpose of this book is to provide a practical, step-by-step approach to creating and using IT service management processes to increase the efficiency and effectiveness of your IT organization. ISO/IEC 20000, the first international standard for IT service management, defines IT service management as follows:

> *IT service management (ITSM) is an integrated process approach that enables an IT organization to deliver services that meet business and customer requirements.*

The focus of ITSM is on managing the full lifecycle of IT services. Its scope does not typically include project or program management, nor does it include application or software development. However, ITSM processes should be designed and implemented in a way that aligns and integrates with the project and program management and the application and software development processes. The consistent use of well-designed and implemented processes enables IT organizations to:

- Align their efforts with business goals
- Ensure compliance with applicable regulatory controls
- Achieve customer and employee satisfaction

Efficient and effective processes enable both customers and IT staff to know *what* needs to be done and *how* things need to be done. This book is designed to help you determine the right ITSM processes to perform, and how to perform them well. It describes how to develop and implement ITSM processes that deliver profound and positive results in the form of business value. It also describes the

1

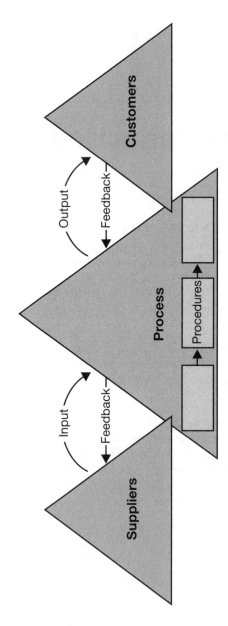

Figure 1.1 Process model (From Knapp, *A Guide to Service Desk Concepts*, 3E. 2010, South-Western, a part of Cengage Learning, Inc. Reproduced by permission. www.cengage.com/permissions)

critical components that must be considered to ensure efficient and effective processes. These critical components are:

- **People**: Individuals and teams who support customers by performing processes
- **Processes**: Interrelated work activities that take inputs and produce outputs that are of value to a customer
- **Technology**: Tools and technologies that people use to do their work
- **Information**: Data and information that people need to do their work, measure process efficiency and effectiveness, and identify improvement opportunities

The focus of this book is on the process component; however, it is impossible to ignore the other components—people, technology, and information—as they ultimately determine how processes are performed. As illustrated in Figure 1.1, processes and procedures exist in every IT organization and in every business:

- A **process** is a collection of interrelated work activities that take a set of specific *inputs* and produce a set of specific *outputs* that are of value to a customer
- A **procedure** is a step-by-step set of instructions that describe how to perform the activities in a process

> *Processes define* what *work to do.*
> *Procedures define* how *to do the work.*

In today's fast-paced business world, every worker is responsible for a process at some level. Furthermore, every worker is simultaneously a **supplier** (or creator) of process input and a **customer** (or recipient) of process output.

To understand the importance of adopting a process-oriented approach, it is useful to discuss the changing role of IT and how business and industry trends are influencing its role.

1.1 The Changing Role of IT

The role of IT has changed dramatically in recent years and organizations can continue to expect significant changes over the next few years. This is because expectations have changed and business leaders expect IT to deliver technology solutions that support top business goals such as[1]:

- Improving business processes
- Cutting enterprise costs

---

[1]IT's Top 10 Business Priorities for 2010, Gartner Inc.

- Increasing the use of information/analytics in decision making
- Improving enterprise workforce effectiveness
- Attracting new and retaining existing customers
- Creating innovative new products and services

Although most of these goals are ever present, business process improvement is a strong trend that requires ongoing collaboration between IT and its business customers. An extension of business process improvement, **business process management (BPM)** is a systematic approach to improving an organization's business processes. BPM goals include:

- Aligning business processes with customer needs
- Improving the organization's ability to achieve its business goals
- Improving the efficiency and effectiveness of business processes
- Enabling agility, innovation, and integration with technology

A **business process** is a set of interrelated activities that accomplish a specific business goal. In other words, it is a process, like any other process. Business processes may include:

- **Core**: The processes that represent an organization's core competency (e.g., manufacturing, financial services, and healthcare). These processes focus on delivering a product or service to the organization's external customers.
- **Supporting**: The processes that govern or control and support business activities (e.g., accounting, corporate governance, human resources, and ITSM).

Many IT organizations view BPM as something "the business does." IT is then engaged after the fact to automate the results. However, IT must be engaged throughout a BPM initiative for a number of reasons including:

1. The IT organization is part of the business and in some cases *is* the business. Whether the IT organization's processes represent the core or supporting processes, the processes used by IT are business processes and must be continually improved.
2. The business and IT must work together to determine where integration, automation, or workflow redesign will improve process efficiency or increase agility.
3. Tools such as those used for process design, modeling, and measurement—which are deployed and maintained by IT—can improve the effectiveness of the process improvement activities themselves.

Having IT engaged in BPM activities ensures that long range goals are understood and that ITSM efforts underpin those goals. Having IT engaged also helps ensure that all options are explored and the best solution(s) are identified. As those options often include contracting with external suppliers or partners to deliver some or all IT services, partners must be engaged during process design and improvement activities as well. Having partners involved ensures roles, responsibilities, and interfaces are clearly understood.

Once viewed as a part of the back office, the IT organization now can—and should—contribute directly to the bottom line. Times have changed and today's IT organization is expected to:

- Deliver value
- Contribute to the achievement of business goals
- Manage and continually improve processes
- Improve regulatory compliance
- Enable innovation
- Understand and reduce costs
- Understand and reduce risks
- Satisfy customers

Customer satisfaction reflects the difference between how a customer expects to be treated and how a customer perceives he or she was treated. This reality is one of the many things that make satisfying customers a challenge. Two people who experience the same event will *perceive* that event differently. What a customer perceives as good one day may not be good enough the next.

> *Clearly defined and optimized processes enable organizations to understand their customers' requirements and manage their customers' expectations.*

1.2 The Importance of IT Service Management Processes

ITSM processes help organizations achieve business and IT alignment, which is a top priority for Chief Information Officers (CIOs) according to a survey conducted by CIO Insight[2].

An integrated approach to implementing ITSM processes also enables IT organizations to balance critical traits such as those illustrated in Table 1.1. All of these traits are important to IT customers and cannot be viewed as mutually exclusive. Balance is important and is achieved by:

1. Rigorously executing processes
2. Measuring and monitoring process performance
3. Continually improving processes

As illustrated in Table 1.2, well-documented and managed ITSM processes enable an organization to change its behaviors and ultimately its culture.

---

[2]CIO Priorities for 2010, The Society for Information Management (SIM)

Table 1.1 Critical traits enabled by processes

Critical process traits	
Efficiency	Effectiveness
Stability	Agility
Standardization	Innovation

Table 1.2 Common IT service management culture shifts

IT service management culture shifts	
• **Reactive**—people simply react to events that occur each day (i.e., "firefighting").	• **Proactive**—people use information to anticipate customer needs (i.e., "fire prevention").
• **People-dependent**—subject matter experts are called upon to handle work activities any hour of the day or night often resulting in lost productivity and burnout.	• **Process-dependent**—knowledge is captured and reused. Roles and responsibilities are clearly defined, resulting in the effective use of subject matter experts and providing growth opportunities.
• **IT-centric**—little understanding of business impact exists and priorities are based on the pain being experienced by IT.	• **Business-centric**—business impact is predefined and business goals are understood. Priorities are based on business impact and need.

The processes that IT organizations perform vary based on factors such as its type (e.g., internal or external service provider), size, and stage of maturity. Business goals and the required level of business and IT integration also influence the processes performed.

1.3 Using Process Frameworks and Standards

Although it is possible to start with a clean sheet of paper when designing or improving a process, it is much more efficient to use an existing framework or standard as a starting point. A **framework** is a logical structure for classifying and organizing complex information. A **process framework** describes best practices that can be used to define and continually improve a given set of processes. Process frameworks also provide a common vocabulary that organizations can use when describing and executing processes.

Because a framework does not contain the mandatory requirements found in a standard, organizations can choose to adopt some practices and not others. This is an important distinction, as organizations often lack the resources required to adopt all of the practices described in a framework, at least initially. For example, the widely used Information Technology Infrastructure Library® framework (discussed below) describes more than 20 processes and hundreds of best practices. Few organizations have the resources to focus on all of these processes at once. Instead, most organizations initially adopt a basic set of practices for a small subset of processes, and expand their use of the framework over time.

> *The term compliant is sometimes erroneously used when discussing frameworks; for example, an organization may say that it is "ITIL®-compliant." A framework is not a standard and thus lacks the mandatory controls needed for an organization to demonstrate compliance.*

The world's largest developer and publisher of international standards is the **International Organization for Standardization (ISO)**. ISO is a network of the national standards institutes of more than 150 countries, one member per country, with a Central Secretariat in Geneva, Switzerland.

In the context of ISO, a **standard** is a document that contains an agreed-upon and approved set of requirements that an organization must satisfy to be certified. ISO standards are created by committees of experts who discuss and debate requirements until a consensus is reached on a draft agreement. Draft agreements are published for public review, and committee members use the feedback they receive to formulate a revised agreement. For an agreement to be accepted as an international standard, it must be voted on and approved by the ISO national members.

ISO standards are voluntary, and organizations can choose to comply with the standards—or not. However, to be certified, an organization must produce evidence that it has put in place all of the mandatory controls specified in the standard. This evidence must be presented to a third-party organization known as a registered certification body during an independent audit. An **audit** is an examination of evidence such as documents and records to verify compliance with a law, regulation, policy, or standard.

> *The ISO/IEC 20000 standard requires evidence of both intentions and activities. Documents provide evidence of intentions and may include policies, plans, procedures, service level agreements, and contracts. Records show evidence of activities and may include audit reports, requests for change, incident records, training records, and invoices sent to customers. The standard specifies that documentation can be in any form or type of medium.*

Achieving ISO certification can cost an organization tens of thousands of dollars and take months of effort. Companies that seek ISO certification typically

Table 1.3 Characteristics of frameworks and standards

Frameworks	Standards
Describe best practices	Define an agreed-upon repeatable way of doing something
Provide guidance and suggestions	Define a formal specification
Support organizations' efforts to design and continually improve processes	Prescribe a minimum set of practices organizations must have in place to assure quality processes
Lack the mandatory controls needed for an organization to demonstrate compliance	List mandatory controls that an organization must show as evidence to be certified

do so to provide their customers assurance that quality processes are used to produce their products and services. ISO certification also enables companies to create a competitive advantage and attract customers. Some organizations are required to achieve ISO certification if they choose to do business with a particular customer or compete in a particular market space. Table 1.3 compares the characteristics of frameworks and standards. Many frameworks and standards exist that enable IT organizations to manage and support information technology and continually improve the quality of their services.

1.4 IT Service Management Frameworks

Several frameworks help clarify the scope of ITSM. These frameworks provide guidance and describe best practices that IT organizations can use to implement and continually improve their ITSM capabilities.

> *A **best practice** is a proven way of completing a task to produce a near-optimum result. Best practices are proven over time through experience and research to work for a large number and variety of people and organizations.*

Many organizations adopt practices from multiple frameworks in an effort to develop a set of processes that meet their needs. The most commonly used ITSM frameworks include:

- Information Technology Infrastructure Library®
- Control Objectives for Information and related Technology
- Microsoft® Operations Framework

The **Information Technology Infrastructure Library®(ITIL®)** is a set of best practice guidance drawn from public and private sectors worldwide that describes a systematic and professional approach to the management of IT services. ITIL was developed in the 1980s by the British Government's Central Computer and Telecommunications Agency, now called the Office of Government Commerce, with the goal of developing a framework for efficient and financially responsible use of IT resources within the British government and the private sector.

Widely adopted in the 1990s, the library has evolved and ITIL Version 3, published in June 2007, consists of five books that span the service lifecycle:

- *Service Strategy*: Provides guidance on how to design, develop, and implement service management. It covers processes such as financial, service portfolio, and demand management.
- *Service Design*: Provides guidance for the design and development of services and service management processes. It covers processes such as service catalog, service level, availability, capacity, IT service continuity, information security, and supplier management.
- *Service Transition*: Provides guidance for the development and improvement of capabilities for transitioning new and changed services into operations. It covers processes such as change, service asset and configuration, release and deployment, and knowledge management. Other processes include transition planning and support, validation and testing, and evaluation.
- *Service Operation*: Provides guidance on achieving effectiveness and efficiency in the delivery and support of services. It includes processes such as event, incident, problem, and access management, along with request fulfillment.
- *Continual Service Improvement*: Provides guidance on creating and maintaining value for customers through better design, transition, and operation of services. It includes processes such as service measurement, service reporting, and the 7-step improvement process.

Control Objectives for Information and related Technology (COBIT®) is an IT governance framework and supporting toolset that allows managers to bridge the gap between control requirements, technical issues, and business risks. Created in 1992 by the Information Systems Audit and Control Association and the IT Governance Institute, the framework continues to evolve and COBIT 4.1 was released in May 2007.

COBIT enables clear policy development and good practice for IT control throughout organizations. COBIT defines IT activities in a generic process model within four domains:

- **Plan and organize:** Covers the use of information and technology and how it can best be used in a company to help achieve the company's goals and objectives

- **Acquire and implement:** Covers identifying IT requirements, acquiring the technology, and implementing it within the company's current business processes
- **Deliver and support:** Focuses on the delivery aspects of the information technology
- **Monitor and evaluate:** Deals with a company's strategy in assessing the needs of the company, and whether or not the current IT system still meets the objectives for which it was designed, and the controls necessary to comply with regulatory requirements

ITIL and COBIT complement each other; for example, you can supplement the IT operational process strengths of ITIL with the critical success factors and key performance indicators of COBIT.

> *A **critical success factor (CSF)** is a measurable characteristic that must exist for a process to be viewed as successful. CSFs reflect the core objectives of a process and support business goals and objectives. A **key performance indicator (KPI)** is a key metric used to manage a process. A **metric** is a performance measure. KPIs underpin critical success factors. Chapter 8 discusses CSFs and KPIs in greater detail.*

The **Microsoft® Operations Framework (MOF)** consists of integrated best practices, principles, and activities that provide comprehensive guidelines for achieving reliability for IT solutions and services. Originally introduced in 1999, the platform-independent framework has evolved and MOF 4.0 was introduced in July 2008. The guidance in MOF encompasses all of the activities and processes involved in managing an IT service: its conception, development, operation, maintenance, and—ultimately—its retirement. MOF organizes these activities and processes into service management functions (SMFs), which are grouped together in phases that mirror the IT service lifecycle. In MOF, the IT service lifecycle is composed of three ongoing phases and one foundational layer that operates throughout all of the other phases. The lifecycle phases are:

- **Plan:** Planning and optimizing the IT service to align with the business strategy
- **Deliver:** Design and delivery of the IT service
- **Operate:** Ongoing operation and support
- **Manage:** Underlying foundation of IT governance, risk management, compliance, team organization, and change management

Each SMF is anchored within a lifecycle phase and contains a unique set of goals and outcomes supporting the objectives of that phase. Management reviews confirm an IT service's readiness to move from one phase to the next. Performing management reviews helps ensure that goals are achieved in an appropriate fashion and that the IT organization's goals are aligned with the goals of the business.

Each of these frameworks—ITIL, COBIT, and MOF—provide certification schemes that are designed to enable organizations to deliver a consistent level of education and recognize the competence of their employees. Where applicable, employing certified professionals helps enable an organization to produce evidence that employees possess the needed knowledge and skills.

1.4.1 Complementary Frameworks

Several vendor-specific frameworks provide tools that organizations can use to speed their process design efforts including:

- **IBM Tivoli Unified Process (ITUP):** A web-based tool that provides detailed documentation of ITSM processes based on industry best practices, including ITIL best practices. ITUP enables organizations to significantly improve IT efficiency and effectiveness by enabling users to easily understand processes, the relationships between processes, and the roles and tools involved in an efficient process implementation.
- **HP Service Management Framework:** A framework that incorporates the major ITSM frameworks and standards—including ITIL, CMMI, ISO/IEC 20000, and ISO/IEC 27001—with the HP Service Management Reference Model, which provides deep-level processes that can be leveraged during process design. The framework provides a common language based on industry best practices and international standards, and can be used as a starting point for building or improving an ITSM system.

These vendor-specific frameworks complement frameworks such as ITIL, COBIT, and ISO/IEC 20000. It is common, in fact, for individuals using these vendor-specific frameworks to pursue certification in one or more of the vendor-neutral frameworks such as ITIL.

What are the minimum ITSM processes required? ISO/IEC 20000 provides a good place to start, and serves as the foundation for the remainder of this book.

1.5 IT Service Management Standard—ISO/IEC 20000

ISO/IEC 20000 is an international standard that promotes the adoption of an integrated process approach to effectively deliver managed services to meet the business and customer requirements.

Introduced in December 2005, ISO/IEC 20000 is the first ITSM process standard to be produced by ISO. ISO/IEC 20000 supersedes British Standard BS 15000. ISO/IEC 20000, like its BS 15000 predecessor, was originally based on best practice guidance contained within the ITIL framework and is expected to stay loosely aligned with ITIL. It equally supports other ITSM frameworks and approaches.

> *ISO/IEC 20000 does not certify the quality of an organization's services or products; it certifies that the organization has effective ITSM processes.*

The ISO/IEC 20000 standard consists of two parts.

- **ISO/IEC 20000-1:** The formal specification defines the requirements—the "shalls"—for an organization to deliver managed services of an acceptable quality for its customers. The scope includes:
  - Requirements for a management system
  - Planning and implementing service management
  - Planning and implementing new or changed services
  - Service delivery processes
  - Relationship processes
  - Resolution processes
  - Control processes
  - Release processes
- **ISO/IEC 20000-2:** The Code of Practice describes best practices—the "shoulds"—for service management processes within the scope of ISO/IEC 20000-1.

> *The Specification and Code of Practice can be used by organizations preparing to be audited against ISO/IEC 20000 or by organizations simply benchmarking their performance and planning service improvements.*

The standard represents the minimum critical activities for achieving ITSM success. It also provides an internationally recognized and tested management system that organizations can use to plan, manage, deliver, monitor, report, review, and improve their IT services.

Organizations seeking the ISO/IEC 20000 certification must provide evidence to an independent auditor that they have fulfilled all of the requirements—the "shalls"—specified in the standard. Other organizations may opt to simply benchmark their processes against the requirements, or provide evidence to only an internal auditor.

Each process discussed in the frameworks above and in the ISO/IEC 20000 standard could be implemented on its own, as each process offers opportunities for improved service management. An integrated process approach, however, offers greater benefits and is necessary to meet the requirements of ISO/IEC 20000. This is because the output from one process provides input into another.

Figure 1.2 illustrates the processes within the scope of the ISO/IEC 20000 standard and their logical groupings. ISO/IEC 20000 process objectives include:

Service Delivery Processes:

- **Service level management:** Define, agree, record, and manage levels of service
- **Service reporting:** Produce agreed, timely, reliable, and accurate reports for informed decision making and effective communication
- **Service continuity and availability management:** Ensure that agreed service continuity and availability commitments to customers can be met in all circumstances
- **Budgeting and accounting:** Budget and account for the cost of service provision
- **Capacity management:** Ensure that the service provider has, at all times, sufficient capacity to meet the current and future agreed demands of the customer's business needs
- **Information security management:** Manage information security effectively within all service activities

Relationship Processes:

- **Business relationship management:** Establish and maintain a good relationship between the service provider and the customer based on understanding the customer and their business drivers
- **Supplier management:** Manage suppliers to ensure the provision of seamless, quality services

Resolution Processes:

- **Incident management:** Restore agreed service to the business as soon as possible or respond to service requests
- **Problem management:** Minimize disruption to the business by proactive identification and analysis of the cause of incidents and by managing problems to closure

Control Processes:

- **Change management:** Ensure all changes are assessed, approved, implemented, and reviewed in a controlled manner
- **Configuration management:** Define and control the components of the service and infrastructure and maintain accurate configuration information

Release Processes:

- **Release management:** Deliver, distribute, and track one or more changes in a release into the live environment

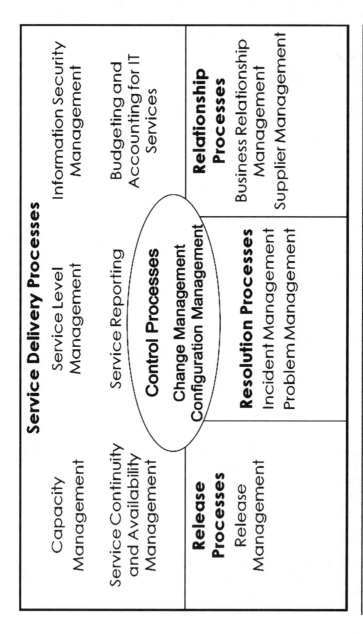

Figure 1.2 ISO/IEC 20000 process model

Each of these processes contributes in some way to the delivery of services that are of value to customers.

1.6 The Value Chain and Its Effect on Processes

The relationship between the internal and external customers of an organization is tightly linked. For example, every interaction the IT service desk or help desk has with an internal customer—i.e., another employee of the company—affects that person's ability to provide excellent service to his or her customers, who may be the external customers of the company.

This concept is known as the service delivery or value chain. First described and popularized by Harvard Business School Professor Michael Porter in his book, *Competitive Advantage: Creating and Sustaining Superior Performance*, a **value chain** categorizes the value-adding activities of an organization and beyond. Analysis enables an organization to "link" together those activities that maximize value creation while minimizing costs.

The simple value chain illustrated in Figure 1-3 shows the relationship that exists between customers, internal service providers, and external service providers. Feedback is used to communicate customer expectations through the value chain. Using the feedback as a guide, internal service providers receive input and deliver output to other service providers, until the expected service is delivered to the customer. Sometimes, external service providers are engaged by internal service providers in an effort to meet the customer's expectations. For example, a service desk analyst or technical specialist may contact a vendor for help resolving a particularly difficult incident. At that point, the internal service provider becomes the vendor's customer. The vendor will have its own value chain that must now work together to meet its customers' expectations.

The value chain illustrates that all of the departments within a company—all of its internal service providers—are interdependent and must work together, and with external suppliers, to deliver services to external customers. Even departments that do not interface directly with customers perform work—in the form of supporting processes—that contributes to the delivery of services to external customers.

> *What is a Value Network? Much of the value that an IT organization creates is intangible and complex. In many cases, value is created through non-linear relationships, as opposed to a simple value chain. A **value network** is a complex set of relationships between two or more individuals, groups, or organizations. **Value network analysis** enables organizations to understand and optimize the relationships within a value network.*

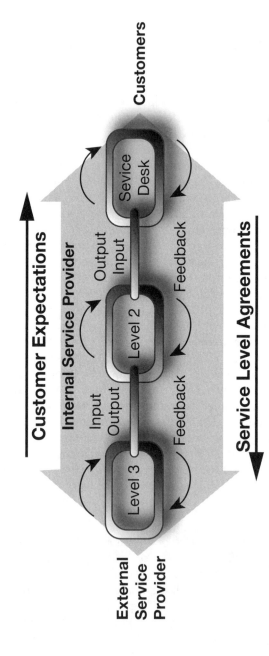

Figure 1.3 Service delivery or value chain (From Knapp, *A Guide to Customer Service Skills for the Service Desk Professional*, 3E. 2011, South-Western, a part of Cengage Learning, Inc. Reproduced by permission. www.cengage.com/permissions)

Processes are the mechanism that enables this creation of value through relationships and ensures customer needs are met. Within processes, everyone can be considered at times a customer and at other times a supplier. For example, a co-worker may ask you to provide information needed to complete a project. In this case, you are the supplier and your co-worker is the customer. Later in the day, you may ask this same co-worker to help you solve an incident. Now you are the customer and your co-worker is the supplier. Whether a customer or a supplier, you must respect the fact that each person you interact with has a role to play—a job to do—and you must strive to understand the other's needs and expectations. Ultimately, the job each of you does leads—via the value chain—to the delivery of service to the company's external customers. As a result, you must strive to understand your external customers' needs and expectations as well as those of your internal customers.

> *Effective process design and continual process improvement ensures that each role in a service delivery chain adds value.*

A hallmark of high-performing organizations is that the processes used to deliver services, including roles and responsibilities, are clearly defined and continually improved. Continual improvement begins with understanding the maturity of your processes.

1.7 Assessing Process Maturity

Process maturity refers to how well a process is defined, how capable it is of being continually improved through the use of measures tied to business goals, and how well it is embedded in the organization's culture.

Many assessment frameworks exist that enable organizations to evaluate process maturity. Assessing process maturity enables organizations to:

- Prioritize improvement efforts
- Set improvement targets
- Avoid the costly implementation of changes that do not address the root cause of process-related problems

The frameworks most commonly used to assess process maturity include:

- **Capability Maturity Model® Integration:** A process improvement approach that provides organizations with the essential elements of effective processes that ultimately improve their performance. CMMI (discussed in greater detail in Chapter 3) is most commonly used to improve software development processes and uses the following scale to assess process maturity:

- o Level 5: Optimizing
- o Level 4: Managed
- o Level 3: Defined
- o Level 2: Repeatable
- o Level 1: Initial

- **ISO/IEC 15504:** An international standard for IT process assessment. ISO/IEC 15504 is also typically used to assess the maturity of software development processes. Formerly known as SPICE (software process improvement and capability determination), ISO/IEC 15504 uses the following scale to assess process maturity:
  - o Level 5: Optimizing
  - o Level 4: Predictable
  - o Level 3: Established
  - o Level 2: Managed
  - o Level 1: Performed
  - o Level 0: Incomplete

- **ITIL Process Maturity Framework (PMF):** A framework that can be used to assess or measure the maturity of ITSM processes. ITIL PMF uses the following scale to assess process maturity:
  - o Level 5: Optimizing
  - o Level 4: Managed
  - o Level 3: Defined
  - o Level 2: Repeatable
  - o Level 1: Initial

Chapter 5 describes techniques for assessing process maturity in greater detail. As the focus of this book is on ITSM processes, the ITIL PMF is used.

Each growth level or stage represents a transformation and requires changes in:

- **Vision and steering:** The communication of goals and allocation of funds and resources
- **People:** Skills and competencies
- **Processes:** Ways of working
- **Technology:** To support and enable the people and processes
- **Culture:** The values and beliefs that prevail and the way in which IT views its relationship with the business, its customers, and IT users

This maturation process takes time and, as the old expression states, "You must take time, to save time." Such is the case with processes. This maturation process also requires a clear understanding of customer requirements or your improvement efforts may be in vain. Chapter 2 describes how to define customer requirements prior to defining processes and how to translate customer requirements into process improvements.

Summary

In today's competitive business climate, IT organizations must do the right things right. IT service management (ITSM) processes enable IT organizations to increase their efficiency and effectiveness. To achieve efficiency and effectiveness, four critical components must be considered: people, processes, technology, and information.

Several frameworks describe best practices IT organizations can use to implement and continually improve their ITSM capabilities. Many organizations adopt and adapt best practices from multiple frameworks in an effort to develop a set of processes that meet their needs. The most commonly used ITSM frameworks are: the Information Technology Infrastructure Library® (ITIL®), Control Objectives for Information and related Technology (COBIT®), and Microsoft® Operations Framework (MOF). Vendor-specific frameworks include: IBM Tivoli Unified Process and HP Service Management Framework.

ISO/IEC 20000, the first international standard for ITSM, promotes the adoption of an integrated process approach to effectively deliver managed services to meet the business and customer requirements. ISO/IEC 20000 provides a good place to start when determining the minimum processes to be implemented. The standard defines requirements—the "shalls"—for an organization to deliver managed services of an acceptable quality for its customers, and also describes best practices—the "shoulds"—for service management processes within its scope.

A value chain categorizes the value-adding activities of an organization and beyond. Processes are the mechanism that enables this creation of value through relationships and ensures customer needs are met. Within processes, everyone can be considered at times a customer and at other times a supplier. High-performing organizations ensure processes are clearly defined and continually improved.

Process maturity refers to how well a process is defined, how capable it is of being continually improved through the use of measures tied to business goals, and how well it is embedded in the organization's culture. Many frameworks exist that enable organizations to assess process maturity. The most commonly used frameworks include: Capability Maturity Model® Integration (CMMI), ISO/IEC 15504, and ITIL Process Maturity Framework (PMF). The maturation of processes takes time and requires a clear understanding of customer requirements or your efforts will be in vain.

Discussion Topics

- IT organizations often look for technological solutions to cultural problems. What are the consequences of failing to consider people, processes, technology, and information when designing and improving ITSM processes?
- Adopting an ITSM framework has its pros and cons. What are the benefits? What are the downsides?

- To continually improve an organization must be willing to assess process maturity. What can go wrong when assessing process maturity? What are lessons learned?

Review Questions

1. List and briefly describe the four critical components that must be considered to ensure efficient and effective processes.
2. What is the difference between a process and a procedure?
3. Why is satisfying customers a challenge?
4. List and briefly describe the three ITSM culture shifts that result from well-documented and managed ITSM processes.
5. How are best practices beneficial to organizations developing processes to meet their needs?
6. Define and briefly describe COBIT.
7. What role do CSFs and KPIs play when designing processes?
8. How is ISO/IEC 20000 different than ITIL?
9. Briefly explain the concept of a value chain.
10. What three criteria determine the maturity of a process?

This book has free material available for download from the
Web Added Value™ resource center at *www.jrosspub.com*

2

Defining and Analyzing
Customer Requirements

Long gone are the days when an employee performs only one single, specialized task. Also gone are the days when employees only need to know the procedures required to complete their portion of a process. Today employees must:

- Understand an entire process
- Clearly understand the expected results of the process
- See where their job fits into the process
- Understand how their contributions work with others to produce the expected results

When employees understand an entire process and the expected results, they can help eliminate bottlenecks and unnecessary tasks that may stand in their way or slow them down. Also, because employees are continuously identifying new customer requirements, employees who are familiar with an entire process can respond quickly to changing customer needs.

An IT organization must manage many tightly integrated processes to meet business goals and achieve customer satisfaction. These processes are integrated because the output produced by one process might be used as input to another process.

For these processes to be successful—and for an IT organization to be successful—business and customer requirements must drive process design and improvement activities.

2.1 Gathering Requirements

By definition, a **requirement** is something that is required; a necessity. A customer requirement, therefore, is a service or level of service that customers feel IT must deliver to facilitate business outcomes. Requirements surface as a result of:

- A consolidation or merger
- The implementation of a new business process
- The need to reduce costs or risks
- The need to increase productivity and quality
- A change in the way your company is doing business
- The need to change the way your company is doing business, caused by:
  o New laws or regulations
  o Increased competition
  o New technology

Ask yourself the following questions:

- Yes or no. Are you delivering effective services that meet your customers' needs?
- Yes or no. Do you really understand your customers' needs and expectations?
- How do you know?
- When was the last time you checked?

The most obvious way to know if you understand and are meeting your customers' needs and expectations is to ask. Conversations with customers can occur informally through one-on-one or "town hall" meetings. Some organizations have business analysts or business relationship managers, also known as account managers, who meet with customers on a regular basis to understand their needs.

More formal techniques that can be used to determine customer requirements include:

- Surveying customers
- Conducting needs assessments
- Creating and using service level agreements
- Benchmarking

2.1.1 Surveying Customers

Customer satisfaction surveys are a series of questions that ask customers to provide their perception of the services being offered. Customer satisfaction surveys are an excellent way to measure the strengths and weaknesses of existing services. Surveys provide insight as to whether customers *perceive* their needs are being met, unlike more quantifiable metrics such as availability and mean time to resolve incidents. Surveys can be conducted during telephone calls, via email, or by asking customers to provide feedback via the web. The two most common customer satisfaction surveys are:

- **Event-driven surveys**: A series of questions that ask customers for feedback on a single, recent service event, such as an incident or service request
- **Overall satisfaction surveys**: A series of questions that ask customers for feedback about all of their interactions with IT during a certain period of time

IT can use the responses to these surveys to identify improvement opportunities and customer requirements, particularly when open-ended questions are included on the survey. For example: "Do you have any comments or suggestions about the services provided by IT?" "How do you feel IT can best support your current and future technology-related needs?"

2.1.2 Conducting a Needs Assessment

Conducting satisfaction surveys, whether annually, or on an ongoing basis, is extremely important and done regularly by world-class organizations.

While some requirements may be gathered when conducting surveys (e.g., by asking customers how they believe the IT organization can improve), sufficient feedback is rarely received to:

- Budget properly for the coming year
- Develop, reengineer, or improve processes
- Plan and execute process improvement projects

This type of data is better collected through a needs assessment. Conducting a needs assessment is important because . . .

> *Customer satisfaction surveys typically ask customers to provide their perception of the services that are being offered. A needs assessment asks customers to provide their expectations relative to the services that are being offered, or that should be offered.*

Techniques that can be used to gather customer requirements during a needs assessment include:

- **Direct interviewing:** Direct interviewing involves meeting with and questioning customers and may include conducting focus groups. You'll want to interview management level decision makers, along with a sampling of representatives from each functional area within your organization (e.g., administration, production, sales and marketing, and support).

| Quick Tips: | Resist the temptation to interview everyone. It will turn into a scheduling nightmare and you may become overwhelmed with all of the information you receive. Prior to conducting the interviews, publish the list of questions you will be asking, and encourage interview participants to solicit the perspective of their employees and co-workers. |
| | Conduct your assessment just prior to your company's annual budgeting process. This will typically ensure participants are sensitive to cost/benefit considerations, and will also enable you to budget appropriately for improvement initiatives. |

- **Documentation review and analysis:** This technique involves studying relevant flowcharts, procedures, forms, job responsibilities, company and departmental objectives, reports, policies, regulations, statistics, etc.
- **Physical review:** Physical review involves formal tours, demonstrations, and informal visits to the various relevant areas.

Although these techniques can be used separately, using all of them together will result in a very complete needs assessment. Table 2.1 provides a step-by-step approach to conducting a needs assessment. Business activity will determine the frequency with which needs assessments are conducted, although at least annually is recommended. During periods of heavy business change, more frequent assessments may be required. Note that in some organizations these activities may be ongoing and performed regularly by a business analyst or business relationship manager.

An effective technique is to prepare and distribute a list of the key questions to be asked in advance of the interview. Figure 2.1 provides a sample email you can send participants prior to their interview.

Interview questions should be primarily open-ended questions. **Open-ended** questions require a greater answer than a single word or two. **Closed-ended** questions prompt a short, single word answer such as "yes" or "no." While you may pose closed-ended questions during the course of the interview (e.g., when asking a follow-up question or when asking for clarification), open-ended questions get people to open up and share their perspective.

Avoid the use of leading questions. **Leading** questions are phrased in such a way that a specific answer is expected (e.g., "The forms on our web site are easy to use, aren't they?"). A better approach is to ask the question in a way that solicits the customer's perception or opinion (e.g., "Do you find the forms on our web site easy to use?").

Here are a few additional interviewing tips:

- Be prepared and on time
- Begin by explaining the meeting purpose and the project goals

Table 2.1 Sample steps for conducting a needs assessment

Conducting a needs assessment
Two to four weeks prior to the assessment
• Establish a high-level interview schedule • Identify interview participants • Develop a detailed interview schedule • Contact each participant to determine/confirm availability • Develop a list of interview questions • Solicit feedback • Refine the list of interview questions
One to two weeks prior to the assessment

• Send an email to each participant that outlines:
  ○ Purpose of the interview
  ○ Agreed upon date and time of the interview
  ○ List of interview questions

During the week(s) of the assessment
• Verify participants' availability (e.g., send a confirmation email a day or two before the interview) • Conduct interviews/gather data • Prepare a requirements definition report • Publish the report • Solicit feedback • Revise the report as needed • Publish the final report • Develop an improvement plan

- Be friendly and courteous; enthusiasm is contagious
- Stress that you are seeking feedback relative to the current environment and the future; avoid letting the interview become a gripe session about the past
- Use open-ended and closed-end questions appropriately
- Avoid leading questions
- Explain terms as needed (e.g., incident or service request)
- Be open minded and receptive to what the customer is saying (even if you disagree)
  - If you're not sure what the customer is saying, ask for an example or re-state what you think was said and ask for clarification

---

<u>Needs Assessment</u>

Date: mm/dd/yy
To: All Stakeholders
From: Project Manager
Subject: Needs Assessment

Information Technology Services (ITS) is currently in the process of assessing and ultimately improving the quality of our services and supporting processes. We are committed to providing the services you need, when you need them.

In the coming weeks we will be conducting a series of interviews aimed at gaining a clear understanding of how ITS can best support your technology needs now and in the future. We greatly appreciate your participation in these interviews.

Attached you will find:
1)   A tentative interview schedule
2)   A list of questions that represent the type of questions you will be asked during the interview. **It is not necessary to complete this questionnaire in advance of the interview.**

The feedback obtained during these interviews will be used as input to an improvement project wherein ITS will refine our internal processes and systems relative to customer support.

The interviews will be conducted by <Date> and we expect these interviews to last one to two hours. We will accommodate your schedule whenever possible.

Please respond to this email by <Date> to verify your availability, establish a meeting site, or reschedule your interview if necessary.

Thank you for taking time to participate in these interviews. Together we can ensure that our company's technology needs are being met.

Figure 2.1   Sample pre-interview email

- If the interview begins to turn into a technical problem-solving session, take a note and assure the customer that you will follow-up on his or her incident after your meeting
- Don't volunteer any results or make any commitments

- If asked about results, indicate you have not finished conducting the interviews or analyzing the information gathered; explain the timeframe and process for communicating results
- Thank participants for their time and if an individual has gone out of their way to be helpful, thank their manager for allowing them to participate

2.1.3 Creating and Using Service Level Agreements

A **service level agreement (SLA)** is a written document that spells out the services that IT will provide the customer, the agreed upon and funded level of service performance, how service performance is measured, and the customer's responsibilities.

The **service level management (SLM)** process is responsible for negotiating SLAs and ensuring agreed upon service levels are met. SLM activities include defining customer requirements, negotiating and agreeing upon the services to be delivered, and perhaps most importantly, managing customer expectations relative to the level of service that IT will provide. A service level manager typically facilitates SLA negotiations between senior management representatives from IT and the business. SLAs are designed to ensure that:

- The IT organization's services match the needs of their customers
- IT and its customers have the same expectations about IT services
- IT and its customers understand their respective responsibilities
- The cost to meet customer expectations does not exceed the benefit that customers will obtain from a service

SLAs ensure that all parties understand and are willing to follow the processes managed by or through the IT organization. SLAs also provide measurable performance metrics relative to those processes.

Since the IT organization is comprised of many departments, and at times relies on the services of external vendors to deliver services, make sure SLAs address the services end-to-end, and that all stakeholders and affected parties are involved in the negotiations. A **stakeholder** is any person or group who is or might be affected by a service, process, or project. Many organizations find operational level agreements and contracts to be extremely useful tools for ensuring that "seamless" service is provided to customers. An **operational level agreement (OLA)** is an agreement between an IT service provider and another part of the same organization. A **contract** is a legally binding agreement between an IT service provider and an external supplier, such as a vendor, contractor, or consultant.

2.1.4 Benchmarking

Benchmarking is the process of comparing an organization's practices and performance metrics to those of another organization—or to industry best practices and industry average metrics—in an effort to identify improvement opportunities.

Companies benefit most from benchmarking when they identify opportunities for improvement, rather than simply comparing metrics. For example, an IT organization can use benchmarking to uncover practices and processes in place at other companies that it can use to improve its own practices and processes. The organization must ensure, however, that any changes it makes in an effort to improve are in line with the needs of *its* customers. In other words, you cannot simply assume that practices and processes that are working at another company will work for your organization.

Organizations sometimes benchmark their processes against best practices in an effort to identify new or innovative processes or concepts that can be used to move their company or department to a position of improved performance. Many think the word innovative simply means "to introduce something new." Innovative can also mean "something newly introduced." The maturity of the organization must be considered. An unsuccessful practice at one point in an organization's maturity may be the right solution at a different point in time. Best practices are best practices for a reason. While not all practices will be right for your organization, strive to understand the "spirit" of the practice before dismissing it all together.

2.2 Translating Customer Requirements

Once information gathering activities such as customer satisfaction surveys and customer needs assessments are complete you will be faced with files full of data that must be translated into customer requirements. Where do you begin? Categorizing the data is a good place to start.

Generally, requirements fall into four familiar categories, and a fifth category you may want to consider. They are:

- People
- Processes
- Technology
- Information
- Marketing/awareness

This fifth category could be used to reflect gaps in the communication and education programs used to manage customer expectations relative to IT services. Communication plans and education and training plans are discussed in greater detail in Chapter 9.

A cause-and-effect diagram, also known as an Ishikawa or fishbone diagram, is a useful tool for categorizing requirements. Cause-and-effect diagrams are discussed in greater detail in chapter 7.

Trends or common needs will become apparent as you are categorizing the data. As these trends emerge you can begin to formulate recommendations. Avoid making conclusive decisions until you have completed all of your analysis.

Sometimes trends are of major importance and require that radical change occur in the form of a reorganization or reengineering initiative. In other cases, it may appear the services currently being offered simply need to be refined, or the skills of the IT staff need to be updated. You may even find that the IT organization has the processes in place that are needed; customers are not just engaged in the processes due to, for example, a bad experience in the past, or a lack of marketing or communication. In that case, increased management involvement or an awareness program may produce the desired results.

Other factors to consider when analyzing the collected data include:

- **Opportunities:** In what areas can IT realize significant improvements or benefits? What specific areas require attention based on your knowledge of similar environments and industry trends? Opportunities may span multiple processes or systems. Opportunities may also focus on management practices, more efficient use of existing IT resources, or more efficient and effective technology and information.
- **Options:** What options are available? There may be more than one option, and each option may contain solutions that span multiple opportunities. The options may be technical, administrative, managerial, organizational, or a combination.
- **Priorities:** As you formulate your recommendations, you may find there are a few that are more relevant, or that will have a greater immediate impact on customer satisfaction. There will be others that will have a minor impact and less of a return on investment or a longer-term impact. Establish a priority scheme such as:
  - Priority 1—High immediate impact, major positive impact on IT performance
  - Priority 2—Medium impact, positive impact on IT performance
  - Priority 3—Low immediate impact, positive longer-term impact on IT performance

Once you have completed your analysis, you can begin to develop a requirements definition document. A **requirements definition document (RDD)** is a formal document that describes the customer and stakeholder requirements for a service, process, or project, along with a recommended solution. An RDD typically includes the following sections:

- Introduction
- Assessment of the current environment
- Requirements (people, processes, technology, information, marketing/awareness)
- Considerations and concerns
- Recommendations
- High-level improvement plan (phase and task definitions, resource requirements, estimated time line)

Taking into consideration the priorities you assigned to your recommendations, prepare your high-level improvement plan. Until the RDD is approved, provide only as much detail as management needs to make a decision. Forward the RDD to all stakeholders and solicit feedback. Revise the document as needed and request final approval. Once approval is obtained to proceed, use proven quality management principles to drive your efforts to develop, reengineer, or improve your ITSM processes.

Summary

Today's employees must understand entire processes, the expected results of processes, and how their contributions work with others to produce those results. A successful IT organization must manage many tightly integrated processes to meet business goals and achieve customer satisfaction. For processes to be successful, business and customer requirements must drive process definition and improvement activities.

A customer requirement is a service or level of service that customers feel IT must deliver to facilitate business outcomes. To ensure you understand and are meeting your customers' needs and expectations you must talk to your customers. Such conversations can occur informally, or using formal techniques such as: surveying customers, conducting needs assessments, creating and using SLAs, and benchmarking.

Once requirements gathering activities are complete, categorizing the data helps to identify and analyze trends or common needs. Common categories include: people, processes, technology, information, and marketing/awareness. As trends or common needs emerge, you can identify opportunities and options, and formulate and prioritize recommendations. Requirements and recommended solutions are documented in an RDD.

Once the document has been reviewed, revised, and approved by all stakeholders, use proven quality management principles to drive your efforts to develop, reengineer, or improve your ITSM processes.

Discussion Topics

- Customer perceptions can vary from day to day and from one situation to the next. Why is it still important to capture customer perceptions?
- Establishing and using service level agreements can be a challenge. What service level management practices and techniques work well? What practices and techniques do not work well?
- When conducting a needs assessment, someone will invariably ask you to share preliminary results or make commitments before all of the interviews are complete. What are the pitfalls of doing so?

Review Questions

1. What is a customer requirement?
2. What is the difference between an event-driven and an overall satisfaction survey?
3. How is conducting a needs assessment different than conducting a satisfaction survey?
4. List and briefly describe three techniques used to gather customer requirements.
5. True or false. During a needs assessment interview, you should only ask closed-ended questions. Explain your answer.
6. Briefly explain two ways that SLAs are beneficial to the management of IT processes.
7. What is benchmarking?
8. What are the five categories used when translating raw customer data into customer requirements?
9. When analyzing customer data and formulating recommendations, how is priority important?
10. What sections are included in a requirements definition document?

This book has free material available for download from the
Web Added Value™ resource center at *www.jrosspub.com*

3

Quality Management Principles

Changing an organization is hard. Even when people are unhappy with the status quo, they tend to hang on to old behaviors and resist even seemingly positive changes. The organization must be ready to change—or you must prepare it to change—or your efforts may be in vain. This is particularly true in the case of re-organizations or reengineering initiatives. Not all organizations are ready for the radical change such initiatives demand. In many cases, radical change isn't even necessary. Before you begin any process-related initiative you must explore:

- The maturity of your organization with regard to process design and improvement
- The willingness of your management team to hold people accountable when processes cross organizational boundaries
- The current culture of your organization (e.g., reactive, proactive, quality-oriented)
- Your organization's ability to absorb change

3.1 Quality Management Basics

Philip B. Crosby—one of the founding fathers of the quality management movement—defines **quality** as conformance to customer requirements. If your company has a quality program in place, you are lucky. Your company has already made a commitment to using processes to ensure its products and services consistently satisfy customer requirements. It is also likely that you have access to resources that can help you develop, reengineer, or improve your processes. These same resources can typically assist you in managing the associated implementation project and in gaining the management commitment you need to be successful.

If your company does not have a quality program in place, you may want to educate yourself about quality principles before you begin. Several quality-related frameworks and standards may be used to drive process design and improvement activities including:

- Total Quality Management
- The Malcolm Baldrige National Quality Award
- Capability Maturity Model® Integration
- Six Sigma
- Lean Six Sigma
- ISO 9000 and ISO 9001

3.1.1 Total Quality Management

In 1950, the Union of Japanese Scientists and Engineers invited Dr. W. Edwards Deming to Japan. He held a series of lectures and seminars during which he taught the basic principles of statistical quality control to executives, managers, and engineers of Japanese industries. His teachings made a deep impression on the participants' minds and provided great impetus in implementing quality control in Japan. The system that the Japanese developed to implement *Kaizen* or continuing improvement through statistical quality control is known as **Total Quality Control (TQC)**. *Kaizen*, when applied to the workplace means continuing improvement involving everyone, managers and workers alike.

> *To this day, the **Deming Prize** is awarded in Japan to companies that have made distinctive improvements in quality or to individuals who have made major contributions to the advancement of quality.*

One of Dr. Deming's best known contributions is the Deming Cycle, illustrated in Figure 3.1. The Deming Cycle is an easy to use model that is particularly relevant to process design and improvement efforts. The **Deming Cycle**—also known as the **PDCA Cycle** (plan, do, check, and act)—is an iterative four-step approach to incremental improvement. A period of consolidation, sometimes also called normalization, allows the changes to become the normal way of working, and prevents the slipping back to old ways.

While its roots are in TQC, a term more commonly used today is **Total Quality Management (TQM)**, which is a management approach to long-term success through customer satisfaction. The term TQM was initially coined by the Naval Air Systems Command to describe its Japanese-style management approach to quality improvement. Since then, TQM has taken on many meanings. TQM is

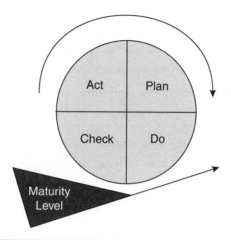

Figure 3.1 The Deming Cycle

based on the participation of all members of an organization in improving processes, products, services, and the culture in which they work. Done well, TQM benefits all members of an organization, and ultimately, society.

> To learn more about TQM, look to the teachings of quality leaders such as Philip B. Crosby, W. Edwards Deming, Armand V. Feigenbaum, Kaoru Ishikawa, and J. M. Juran.

As illustrated in Figure 3.2, TQM serves as an excellent foundational layer for process design and improvement activities. TQM's principles—conformance to customer requirements and ongoing incremental improvement—support and enhance the principles and best practices reflected in any or all of the ITSM and quality management frameworks and standards that an organization may choose to adopt.

3.1.2 Malcolm Baldrige National Quality Award

Many companies show their commitment to TQM by striving to receive the Malcolm Baldrige National Quality Award. The United States Congress established the Malcolm Baldrige National Quality Award in 1987 to recognize U.S. organizations for their achievements in quality and business performance, and to raise awareness about the importance of quality and performance excellence as a competitive edge. The award is not given for specific products or services. Rather, it is given to organizations that are committed to delivering ever-improving value to

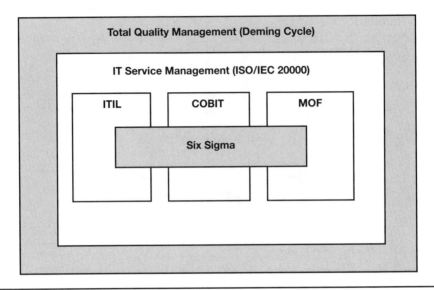

Figure 3.2   TQM as a foundational layer

customers and improving overall organizational performance. Three awards may be given annually in each of these categories: manufacturing, service, small business, education, health care, and nonprofit.

The **Malcolm Baldrige Criteria for Performance Excellence** is a framework of management practices that organizations can use to measure and improve their overall performance. Seven categories make up the award criteria. They are:

- **Leadership:** Examines how senior executives guide the organization and how the organization addresses its responsibilities to the public and practices good citizenship.
- **Strategic planning:** Examines how the organization sets strategic directions and how it determines key action plans.
- **Customer and market focus:** Examines how the organization determines requirements and the expectations of customers and markets.
- **Measurement, analysis, and knowledge management:** Examines the management, effective use, and analysis of data and information to support key organization processes and the organization's performance management system.
- **Workforce Focus:** Examines how the organization enables its workforce to develop its full potential and how the workforce is aligned with the organization's objectives.
- **Process Management:** Examines aspects of how key production/delivery and support processes are designed, managed, and improved.

- **Results:** Examines the organization's performance and improvement in its key business areas: customer satisfaction, financial and marketplace performance, human resources, supplier and partner performance, and operational performance. This category also examines how the organization performs relative to its competitors.

The criteria are used by thousands of organizations of all kinds for self-assessment and training and as a tool to develop performance and business processes.

3.1.3 Capability Maturity Model® Integration

Capability Maturity Model® Integration (CMMI) is a process improvement approach developed and owned by the Software Engineering Institute (SEI). CMMI provides organizations with the essential elements of effective processes that ultimately improve their performance. The SEI offers a number of Capability Maturity Models to assist organizations in maturing their people, process, and technology assets in an effort to improve long-term business performance.

CMMI Version 1.2 was introduced in February 2009 and provides three models that can be used to guide process improvement across a project, a division, or an entire organization. The three models include:

- **CMMI for Acquisition:** Provides best practices for improving relationships with suppliers
- **CMMI for Development:** Focuses on process improvement in development organizations
- **CMMI for Services:** Provides guidance that service providers can use to establish, manage, and deliver services

CMMI for services (CMMI-SVC) draws on concepts and best practices from frameworks and standards such as ITIL, ISO/IEC 20000, and COBIT. It makes it possible for organizations to seamlessly integrate CMMI for development, with other frameworks and standards for service delivery. CMMI-SVC is not designed, however, just for IT services. It is designed to allow for a wide range of services. It is also designed to provide a clear improvement path that organizations can use to increase their capability.

As discussed in Chapter 1, the CMMI maturity models enable organizations to baseline their performance against five maturity levels:

- **Level 5—Optimizing:** Continuous process improvement is enabled by quantitative feedback from the process and by piloting innovative ideas and technologies
- **Level 4—Managed:** Detailed process and quality measures are collected
- **Level 3—Defined:** Processes are documented, standardized, and integrated
- **Level 2—Repeatable:** Basic processes are established and the necessary process discipline is in place to repeat earlier successes

- **Level 1—Initial:** Processes are characterized as ad hoc and occasionally even chaotic; few processes are defined and success depends on individual efforts and heroics

3.1.4 Six Sigma

Six Sigma is a disciplined, data-driven approach and methodology for eliminating defects in any process. The fundamental objective of the Six Sigma methodology is the implementation of a measurement-based strategy that focuses on process improvement and variation reduction through the application of Six Sigma improvement projects. This is accomplished through the use of two Six Sigma sub-methodologies: DMAIC and DMADV.

Six Sigma DMAIC is used to incrementally improve processes that are failing to meet performance specifications. DMAIC steps include:

- Define
- Measure
- Analyze
- Improve
- Control

Six Sigma DMADV is used to develop new processes or products at Six Sigma quality levels. DMADV can also be used for incremental process improvement. DMADV steps include:

- Define
- Measure
- Analyze
- Design
- Verify

Six Sigma processes are executed by certified professionals that hold distinctions such as Six Sigma Green Belt and Six Sigma Black Belt. Six Sigma Master Black Belts oversee process execution activities.

> *The ITIL 7-step improvement process is loosely based on Six Sigma principles.*

3.1.5 Lean Six Sigma

Lean Six Sigma combines the concepts of Lean Manufacturing and Six Sigma. Lean Manufacturing focuses on removing *waste* and improving the flow of processes and procedures. Six Sigma focuses on reducing *defects* by measuring standard deviations from an expected norm. Lean Six Sigma is metric driven, relying on critical success factors and key performance indicators. The Six Sigma DMAIC process is an active component of Lean Six Sigma.

3.1.6 ISO 9000 and ISO 9001

ISO 9000 is a set of universal standards for a quality management system that is accepted around the world. Formulated and maintained by the International Organization for Standardization, ISO 9000 describes quality management fundamentals and offers a common vocabulary. The most comprehensive of the standards is ISO 9001. It describes requirements for a **quality management system (QMS)**, which is a framework for continual quality improvement. QMS requirements include:

- A set of procedures that cover all key processes in the business
- Monitoring processes to ensure they are effective
- Keeping adequate records
- Checking output for defects, with appropriate and corrective action where necessary
- Regularly reviewing individual processes and the QMS itself to ensure continual improvement

While ISO 9000 was initially viewed as a requirement only for manufacturing companies, a variety of organizations now accept and use it to demonstrate their commitment to quality.

To become certified, companies must document and distribute their processes in a manner that conforms to the ISO standards. Companies must provide their employees training in the documented processes, and must be able to demonstrate through a series of quality audits that they are performing the processes as documented. Companies must also provide evidence of continual improvement.

Becoming certified is hard work, but ISO 9000 certified companies typically experience dramatic reductions in customer complaints, significant reductions in operating costs, and increased demand for their products and services.

The ITSM standard ISO/IEC 20000 reflects aspects of ISO 9000 and ISO 9001 as it describes requirements for a management system. This includes policies and a framework to enable the effective management and implementation of all IT services. Requirements specified include:

- **Management responsibility:** Evidence of top/executive management's commitment to developing, implementing, and improving the organization's service management capability (e.g., documented policies, objectives, and plans)
- **Documentation requirements:** Documents and records to ensure effective planning, operation, and control of ITSM activities (e.g., documented policies, plans, processes, procedures, and SLAs)

- **Competence, awareness, and training:** Defined roles and responsibilities, maintained together with required competencies such as training needs

> *What is awareness? ISO/IEC 20000 states that top management shall ensure its employees are aware of the relevance and importance of their activities and how they contribute to the achievement of ITSM objectives.*

3.2 Process Design Considerations

Whether your company is striving to receive the Malcolm Baldrige National Quality Award, achieve the CMMI Optimizing level, become ISO 9000 certified, or "simply" trying to implement quality processes, it is important to note that the process maturity lifecycle reflected in these various frameworks and standards is essentially the same. Processes must be:

- Defined
- Documented
- Managed via performance metrics
- Continually improved

Failing to recognize the effort required to complete these seemingly simple steps is a common mistake that organizations make. Failing to establish clear and measurable improvement targets is another common mistake. Setting improvement targets and selecting a process design approach (discussed below) begins with understanding the factors triggering a process design or improvement initiative.

Common reasons to undertake such an initiative include:

- New or changing customer requirements
- Customer dissatisfaction
- Staff dissatisfaction
- High cost
- Poor quality
- Process takes too long or is too complex
- Process is being circumvented
- Excessive rework or redundant efforts
- Inadequate measures or controls
- Too many or too few signoffs or handoffs
- Job consolidation
- Inadequate data or data redundancy

Understanding why a process design initiative is needed is an excellent place to start. These factors can also be used as input when prioritizing your efforts.

A process improvement priority matrix such as the one illustrated in Table 3.1 can be used to rate process improvement opportunities and create a prioritized list of processes for planning purposes. A **process improvement priority matrix** maps processes eligible for design or improvement against improvement criteria. The criteria is rated using a scale where, for example, one indicates the least opportunity for improvement and five indicates the greatest opportunity for improvement. The "available resources" category is used to reflect the existence of resources such as funding, skilled staff, and technology.

> *Many organizations find that simply identifying pain points and seeking to understand the causes of those pain points provides the insight needed to establish priorities.*

Once priorities are established, one of the following three approaches may be considered:

- **Developing processes:** Documenting and designing processes not previously defined
- **Reengineering processes:** Radically redesigning or reengineering existing processes
- **Improving processes:** Refining existing processes to enhance performance and ensure continual improvement

Table 3.1 Sample process improvement priority matrix

Process improvement priority matrix Scale: 1 = least opportunity for improvement; 5 = greatest opportunity for improvement			
Process	**Incident mgmt**	**Problem mgmt**	**Change mgmt**
Customer dissatisfaction	5	3	4
Employee dissatisfaction	4	4	5
Cost-saving opportunity	2	5	2
Time-saving opportunity	3	3	4
Quick win opportunity	4	5	1
Available resources	5	1	2
Total score	23	21	18

3.2.1 Developing Processes

Developing processes essentially involves starting from scratch. It involves putting down on paper a process that has not previously been documented. The process could be an existing process that has never been formally defined, or it could be a new process that is now needed. When developing a process, keys to success include:

- An accountable process owner
- A dedicated process improvement team
- Participation by all process stakeholders in process development activities
- The identification of customer requirements
- The definition of process goals and performance metrics
- A willingness on the part of management to hold people accountable to the defined process
- A commitment to continually improve the process

> *Evidence that these success factors have been addressed is documented in the form of a process definition document.*

Processes are typically developed in a workshop setting. During the workshop, process stakeholders participate in a series of exercises designed to assist in the definition of the selected process. Because all of the stakeholders are engaged at one time, a workshop can considerably reduce the time required to define a process and begin planning its associated implementation effort. The keys to a successful process definition workshop are:

- A strong facilitator trained in facilitation techniques. Preferably someone who is capable of being neutral when it comes to making decisions. A **Certified Process Design Engineer (CPDE)®** may serve in this capacity. A CPDE is a qualified professional who oversees process design and improvement activities and ensures processes satisfy customer requirements.
- Decision makers who represent each stakeholder group. The participation of decision makers is essential or the process definition process will be considerably prolonged. If the person participating in the workshop must receive permission from his or her boss before making a commitment, he or she is the wrong person for the workshop.

When defining an existing process (i.e., one that is being performed but has never been documented), an effective and common practice is to develop "as is" and "to be" flowcharts:

- A **flowchart** is a detailed diagram that uses standardized symbols, interconnected with lines, to show the successive steps in a process

- An **"as is" flowchart** shows a process as it is currently being performed (whether good, bad, or ugly)
- A **"to be" flowchart** shows how a new process is to be performed once implemented

Creating "as is" and "to be" flowcharts is an excellent technique as project planning activities can focus on the "the gap." In other words, your project plan will define the activities that must occur to analyze and bridge the gap between the current process and the new process.

> *Chapter 7 describes flowcharting and other process mapping techniques in greater detail.*

3.2.2 Reengineering Processes

In the 1980s, Michael Hammer coined the term reengineering. By definition, **reengineering** is the fundamental rethinking and radical redesign of business processes to achieve dramatic improvements in critical, contemporary measures of performance, such as cost, quality, service, and speed.

Wow! What a mouthful. What is so important about this definition is what is not being said. This definition does not say make incremental improvements to an existing process. This definition does not say make changes to parts of your processes but leave their basic structures intact. It basically says . . . *start over*; fundamentally rethink the way you are doing things.

Another term commonly used is **business process reengineering (BPR)**, which is the critical analysis and radical redesign of existing business processes to achieve breakthrough improvements in performance measures.

It should go without saying that no one department, such as IT, or no one team or function within a department, such as the service desk, can "reengineer" on its own. This is because every department and function within an organization has a relationship with other departments and functions. Furthermore, multiple processes may span these various functions. Any organization that radically rethinks the way it performs certain processes must consider how the changes will affect all of the stakeholders in those processes, along with those of any interfacing processes.

> *To ensure all stakeholders are engaged, processes are typically redesigned or reengineered in a workshop setting.*

Although TQM and BPR represent two extremes of the improvement spectrum, both stress the importance of considering the cross-functional impact of process changes. TQM tends to focus on incremental change and gradual improvement of processes. BPR seeks radical redesign and drastic improvement of processes. Redesigning or reengineering processes is hard and is not something an organization should enter into without fully understanding and being committed to the desired final outcome.

Here are some of the common reasons that companies begin a process redesign or reengineering initiative:

- Completely abandon old systems and establish more efficient, effective ways to work (e.g., a best practice framework)
- Empower workers to make decisions
- Combine several jobs into a single job
- Eliminate or reduce handoffs, checks, and controls
- Provide for multiple versions of a process (e.g., triage processes)
- Have work performed where it makes the most sense (e.g., move all customer-related activities to the service desk to provide a single point of contact)
- Perform the steps in a process in a more natural or logical order
- Establish global or enterprise-wide processes (e.g., a single problem management process for global support or a single IT service continuity management process that provides for localized procedures)

Management commitment is an important factor in any process-related initiative. In the case of a process redesign or reengineering initiative, it is vital. This is because management must be willing to adopt the new processes in what may be new departments or teams. They must hold their people accountable to the new processes until those processes become the corporate culture, and they must be willing to empower their employees to make decisions and recommendations as needed for the organization to continually improve.

In an organization where managers are hesitant to give up or share responsibility, where managers micro-manage their staff, or where managers want to be viewed as the "king" or "queen" and are unwilling to embrace any challenges to their turf, process redesign or reengineering initiatives will represent a long, hard, uphill battle.

3.2.3 Improving Processes

Philip B. Crosby's definition of quality—conformance to customer requirements—brings us full circle. In order to define quality processes you must understand your customers' requirements. As customer requirements change, so too must your processes.

Customer requirements, like customer expectations, represent a moving target. One of the reasons customer requirements are a moving target is that as an organization improves the quality of its services, the standard of what constitutes quality gets redefined. Another reason is that as business needs change, service-related needs change. For example, if a division of your company begins offering services Monday through Saturday, as opposed to Monday through Friday, it is likely they will expect the IT organization to begin working on Saturday as well.

To continually improve processes you must:

- Collect and review process performance metrics
- Compare process performance to your customers' requirements
- Identify improvement opportunities such as:
  - Clarifying roles and responsibilities
  - Identifying and eliminating any inefficient or ineffective activities
  - Identifying and implementing enabling technologies
  - Refining existing and implementing additional metrics
- Assign a priority to each improvement opportunity
- Initiate improvement projects based on the priorities assigned to each improvement opportunity
- Begin again . . .

> *Chapter 8 describes performance measurement systems and metrics in greater detail.*

Of the three activities discussed in this section—developing, reengineering, and improving processes—improving processes can actually be the most difficult. This is because once you have the skills, developing processes is easy. You get to start with a clean sheet of paper and figure out the most efficient and effective way to perform a process. Reengineering processes can be a challenge because of all the organizational change issues; however, given the right conditions it is a very exciting time for most organizations. You get to eliminate obstacles that may have long been in your way and create a new way of working.

Incremental improvement is tough. Squeaking out one or two percentage points of improvement often requires imagination and enthusiasm. Furthermore, once an organization achieves world-class status, who does it benchmark against to improve performance?

The biggest mistake an organization can make is to believe their process improvement efforts are "done." Another mistake is to believe that because goals are being consistently met, there is no need to improve. Processes are never done and customer perception will quickly wane if their expectations—requirements—are not continuously identified and met . . . or better yet, exceeded.

In today's competitive climate, companies cannot afford to waste resources. They cannot afford to redo work because it wasn't done right the first time. They have to maximize their resources and ensure that people are doing the right things as efficiently and effectively as possible.

With processes, work is clearly defined, roles and responsibilities are clearly defined, and people understand what they are expected to do. With processes, accurate data is captured in a meaningful and useful way. Through analysis, this data becomes information and knowledge that enables the organization to transform its culture and achieve its goals.

The bottom line is while radical redesign is not always necessary, all IT organizations must define, document, and continually improve processes in an effort to meet or exceed their customers' expectations.

> *Neglected world-class processes will quickly become mediocre. Undefined processes never become world class.*

Summary

Changing an organization is hard. The organization must be ready to change, or you must prepare it to change, or your efforts may be in vain. Before beginning a process-related initiative, consider your organization's maturity with regard to process design and improvement, management's willingness to hold people accountable to processes, your organization's culture, and its ability to absorb change.

Several quality-related frameworks and standards may be used to drive process definition and improvement activities. Examples include: Total Quality Management, the Malcolm Baldrige National Quality Award, Capability Maturity Model® Integration, Six Sigma, Lean Six Sigma, ISO 9000, and ISO 9001.

ISO 9001 describes requirements for a quality management system, which is a framework for continual quality improvement. ISO/IEC 20000 reflects aspects of ISO 9000 and ISO 9001 as it describes requirements for a management system. This includes policies and a framework to enable the effective management and implementation of IT services. Requirements specified include: management responsibilities, documentation requirements, and competence, awareness, and training.

The process maturity lifecycle reflected in each of these frameworks and standards is essentially the same. Processes must be defined, documented, managed via performance metrics, and continually improved. Failing to recognize the effort required to complete these steps is a common mistake, as is failing to establish clear and measurable improvement targets.

Setting improvement targets and selecting a process design approach begins with understanding why a process design initiative is needed. These factors can also be used as input when prioritizing your efforts. A process improvement priority matrix maps processes eligible for design or improvement against improvement criteria. The criteria are rated to determine the greatest opportunity for improvement. Identifying pain points and seeking to understand the causes of those pain points can also provide the insight needed to establish priorities.

Once priorities are established, one of three approaches may be considered: developing, reengineering, or improving processes. Processes are typically developed in a facilitated workshop designed to engage, at one time, decision makers who represent all stakeholder groups. To develop an existing but previously undocumented process, begin by documenting the "as is" process, and then design a "to be" process. Compare the two and then identify ways to bridge the gaps. Use a process definition document to record workshop and process design and improvement results.

Redesigning or reengineering processes involves fundamentally rethinking the processes in an effort to achieve dramatic improvements. No one department or no one team or function can "reengineer" on its own. Process interfaces must be considered. To ensure all stakeholders are engaged, processes are typically redesigned or reengineered in a workshop setting.

Improving processes involves continually collecting and reviewing performance metrics, comparing process performance to customer requirements, and identifying, prioritizing, and initiating improvement projects. Incremental improvement is tough; however, the biggest mistake an organization can make is to believe their process improvement efforts are "done."

Discussion Topics

- Factors such as organizational maturity and culture can greatly impact process design and improvement activities. What factors influence organizational maturity and culture?
- There are several quality-related frameworks and standards available. Should an organization adopt multiple frameworks and standards or just one?
- Organizations often take a "one size fits all" approach to process design and improvement activities. What are the pitfalls of doing so?

Review Questions

1. What four things should you explore before beginning a process-related initiative?
2. Define the term quality.
3. What are two principals of TQM?
4. How is the Deming Cycle relevant to process design and improvement?
5. True or false. The Malcolm Baldrige National Quality Award is given for an organization's products and services. Explain your answer.

6. What is the difference between Six Sigma and Lean Six Sigma?
7. How will attaining an ISO 9000 certification lead to an improvement in an organization's processes?
8. What four characteristics must all processes have according to the various frameworks and standards discussed in this chapter?
9. What are the benefits of using a process design workshop when developing and redesigning processes?
10. What is the difference between reengineering a process and improving a process?

WAV Web
Added
Value™

This book has free material available for download from the
Web Added Value™ resource center at *www.jrosspub.com*

4

Defining and Documenting Processes

People often visualize a flow chart when they hear the word "process." A well-documented process, however, has six key components. They are:

1. **Policies:** A **policy** is a formal document that describes the overall intentions and direction of a service provider, as expressed by senior management. Processes may have process-specific policies, and an organization may have an overall quality management and ITSM policies. Process-specific policies must be compatible with the organization's overall policies.

2. **Overview:** A brief narrative description of the process, along with its objectives and goals. An **objective** is an intended result (i.e., a purpose). A **goal** is a targeted result. Goals should be specific, measurable, achievable, realistic, and timely (SMART). The overview begins to introduce the process's vocabulary and typically contains statements that begin as follows:

   o <Process Name> is the process of . . .
   o The objective(s) of < Process Name> is (are) to . . .
   o The goal(s) of < Process Name> is (are) to . . .

   The process overview also provides information such as the process owner, the process's boundaries, triggers, inputs, suppliers, high-level activities, outputs, customers, and metrics. A **trigger** is an event that initiates, or triggers, the start of a process (e.g., a call to the service desk triggers the incident management process). Metrics are used to evaluate process performance characteristics such as efficiency, effectiveness, cost, and quality.

3. **Roles and Responsibilities**: The roles required to perform a process and the activities or tasks performed by each role. It describes the roles and responsibilities of the process's customers and suppliers.

4. **Process Maps:** A **process map** is a diagram that shows the sequence of tasks that occur within a process and also the relationship a process has with other processes. Process maps (discussed in chapter 7) can take many forms including:

   o High-level integration maps
   o Relationship maps
   o Cross-functional maps
   o Flowcharts

5. **Activities:** The **activities**, or units of work, to be performed within the boundaries of the process or sub-process. Activities are typically converted into procedures or work instructions.

6. **Vocabulary:** The words and phrases to be used when performing and discussing a process. A process's vocabulary is typically presented in the form of a glossary of terms.

There is a subtle difference between *defining* and *designing* a process. Defining a process involves determining its boundaries; in other words, where the process starts, and where it stops. This is an important step as it helps to clarify the purpose of the process, along with its objective(s). It also helps ensure process design activities exclude activities that are the responsibility of another process. For example, in IT it is common for organizations to combine the incident and problem management processes, or the change and release management processes. The end result is often a process that is inefficient, ineffective, confusing in terms of its purpose and objectives, and far more complex than is practical.

> *Once the boundaries of a process are defined, process design activities determine what work to do within those boundaries.*

When a process is exceptionally complex, a good practice is to define subprocesses. A **sub-process** is a logically grouped lower-level view of activities performed within a process. Sub-processes typically represent the three to five key activities to be performed within the boundaries of the process. Each sub-process will have its own triggers, inputs, suppliers, activities, outputs, customers, and metrics, along with its own flowchart.

A **process definition document (PDD)** is a formal document used to record and maintain the details of all process components. Appendix A provides a sample PDD for one of an IT organization's most critical processes—incident management.

4.1 Distinguishing Policies, Processes, Procedures, and Plans

A common debate is whether a "top-down" or "bottom-up" approach works best when designing and implementing processes. While staff buy-in is critical and is discussed in detail in Chapter 9, designing processes must begin at the top with a clear understanding of management's vision.

This statement is not meant to undermine the importance of "grass roots" acceptance of ITSM and the need for enthusiastic change agents within all levels of the organization. Strong leadership—where senior management demonstrates its commitment through words and deeds—is optimal. In the absence of management commitment, enthusiastic change agents can initiate new ideas and introduce best practices where possible. Such efforts, particularly when coupled with quick wins, often result in management becoming more engaged and more clear in terms of stating its vision.

Management's vision is typically expressed in the form of policies, which are then used to create processes, procedures, and plans. Simply put, policies, processes, procedures, and plans are all documents that must be controlled and managed. Document version control and management best practices are discussed in chapter 6. So how are these documents different? Each plays a specific role in a quality management system framework.

Policies, which may also be called principles, standards, or business rules, reflect management's expectations and intentions and are used to:

- Guide decisions
- Guide actions towards a desired outcome
- Develop processes and procedures

To be effective, policies must be:

- Specific
- Measurable
- Underpinned by processes

Processes provide a "big picture" view of the work that people do in support of policies. Procedures underpin processes and provide instructions for how work gets done. Work instructions are linked to procedures when more detailed or localized instructions are needed for performing a single task.

A **work instruction** is a detailed set of instructions that describe how to perform a single task. A **task** is a piece of work assigned to a single individual. If a process involves only a few tasks, the work instructions can be included within procedures. For more complex processes, it may be useful to create higher level procedures and more detailed work instructions where needed. Doing so makes it possible for workers with varying skills to obtain information at the level of detail they need.

Procedures and work instructions are important; however, policies and processes are what enable people to know the expected results of their efforts. By understanding an overall process—all of the procedures that must be performed to produce a result—people can better understand the importance of completing their assigned procedures.

A **plan** is a formal, approved document that describes the capabilities and resources needed to achieve a desired result. Plans are often produced in conjunction with an organization's annual budgeting cycle. Like processes, plans must reflect policies and may include:

- ITSM plan
- Process-specific plans linked to the ITSM plan
- Service improvement plans linked to the ITSM and process-specific plans

Plans are critical and together with policies provide a roadmap to be used when executing projects, such as process design and improvement projects.

According to *A Guide to the Project Management Body of Knowledge* (PMBOK® Guide) published by the Project Management Institute, a **project** is a temporary endeavor undertaken to create a unique product, service, or result. A project has an agreed start and end date, an established budget, and a clearly defined scope of work to be performed.

Policies, processes, procedures, plans, and projects . . . how can an organization integrate these concepts and keep the hierarchy—as illustrated in Figure 4.1—intact? Many organizations initiate a program.

A **program** is a group of related projects managed in a coordinated way to obtain benefits that cannot be achieved by managing the projects individually. A primary benefit is typically the attainment of strategic business outcomes or goals. Other benefits may include economies of scale, standardization, increased control, and reduced costs and risks. **Program management** is the process of managing a group of related projects in a coordinated way to achieve the program's strategic goals and benefits. Program management provides a layer above project management aimed at ensuring:

- Interdependent projects are coordinated
- Interdependent projects reflect management's strategic vision
- Project overlaps are minimized
- Project gaps are minimized

Within individual projects, a project management office may provide guidance. A **project management office (PMO)** is a group or department that centralizes, coordinates, and oversees the management of projects, programs, or a combination of both. The primary goal of a PMO is to achieve benefits by standardizing project management policies, processes, and methods. As is the case with ITSM, a PMO typically bases its project management practices on an industry standard methodology such as the PMBOK® or Projects in Controlled Environments, Version 2 (PRINCE2™).

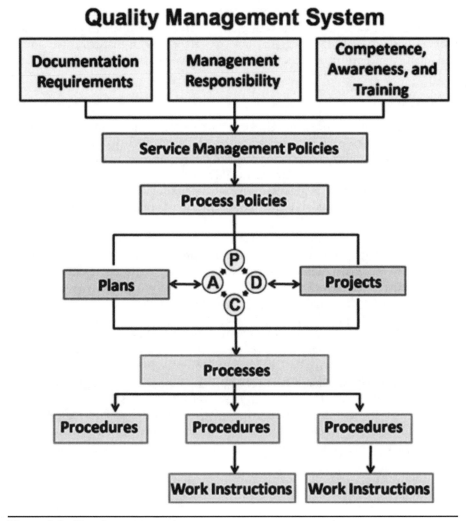

Figure 4.1   Top-down approach

Many organizations establish an ITSM program that coordinates ITSM-related planning activities and oversees:

- Curriculum development and training activities (people)
- Process design and improvement projects (processes)
- Process automation projects (technology)
- Management reporting activities (information)

To ensure program goals are communicated in a consistent and positive way, an ITSM program can initiate marketing and awareness campaigns, perhaps via a theme or brand. An ITSM program can also oversee process maturity assessments and identify and prioritize needed process improvements.

Summary

A well-documented process has six key components: policies, an overview, roles and responsibilities, process maps, activities, and a vocabulary. When a process is exceptionally complex, a good practice is to define sub-processes.

Although "grass roots" acceptance of ITSM is important and necessary, designing processes must begin with an understanding of management's vision. Policies reflect that vision and must be specific, measurable, and underpinned by processes.

Processes provide a "big picture" view of the work that people do in support of policies. Procedures underpin processes and provide instructions for how work gets done. Work instructions are linked to procedures when more detailed or localized instructions are needed.

Plans describe the capabilities and resources needed to achieve a desired result. Together with policies, plans provide a roadmap to be used when executing projects. Many organizations initiate a program to manage one or more interdependent projects. A PMO may provide guidance and help standardize project management policies, processes, and methods.

Many organizations establish an ITSM program that coordinates ITSM-related planning activities. An ITSM program may oversee activities such as: curriculum development and training activities (people), process design and improvement projects (processes), process automation projects (technology), and management reporting activities (information).

Discussion Topics

- Management commitment is critical when designing and improving processes. What are the symptoms of a lack of management commitment?
- A process definition document is a "living" document. When and how should this document be used?
- Processes often become bureaucratic because they are designed without policies. What are other causes of bureaucracy and how can they be avoided?

Review Questions

1. List and briefly describe the six key components of a well-documented process.
2. What is the difference between an objective and a goal?
3. Define the term trigger and provide two examples.
4. How are process metrics used?
5. What are two benefits of process maps?
6. What are sub-processes and when might they be necessary?
7. True or false. A bottom-up approach works best when designing and implementing processes. Explain your answer.
8. Briefly describe the relationship between policies, processes, procedures, and plans.
9. What is a project?
10. Why might an organization establish an ITSM program?

 Web Added Value™

This book has free material available for download from the
Web Added Value™ resource center at *www.jrosspub.com*

5

Assessing Process Maturity

The easiest way to doom a process is to consider it "done." This is because organizations are rarely able to withstand the culture change required to move from having no process to having a high-performing process in a short period of time. It is also uncommon for organizations to have all of the components of a successful process—people, processes, technology, and information—in place and in a mature state when a process is first being designed and implemented. A far better approach is to recognize that organizations and processes mature over time. In other words, they must be continually improved.

The term *continual* improvement is being used in lieu of continuous in recognition of the fact that organizations rarely focus on process improvement in an uninterrupted or *continuous* manner. This is because few IT organizations have the resources to focus both on continuous process improvement and, more importantly, delivering services that meet the needs of the business. It is also important to understand that each level of maturity forms a foundation for the next. Incremental or continual improvement ensures a solid foundation is in place before attempting the next level of maturity. Attempting to skip levels invariably leads to false starts, disappointing results, and decreased morale. Other effects may include cynicism, skepticism, loss of sponsorship, and loss of funding. A far more effective approach is to use the ten process design and improvement steps (discussed in Chapter 6) to *continually* improve.

Recall that process maturity refers to how well a process is defined, how capable it is of being continually improved through the use of measures tied to business goals, and how well it is embedded in the organization's culture. In the case of ITSM processes, process maturity refers to how well a process is embedded in the organization's culture with respect to ITSM.

A cornerstone of continual process improvement is assessing the current level of maturity and determining the steps that must be taken to move to the next

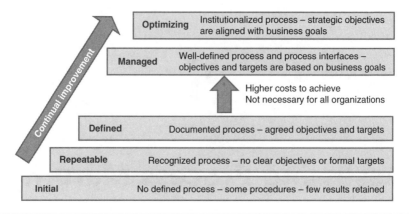

Figure 5.1   ITIL Process Maturity Framework (PMF)

maturity level. As discussed previously, there are many models that can be used to assess process maturity such as CMMI, ISO/IEC 15504, and the ITIL Process Maturity Framework (PMF) (see Figure 5.1). These models are similar in that each describes characteristics and provides a context for measuring process maturity.

For the purposes of this book, the ITIL PMF is being used as a starting point, as it was designed specifically for use with ITSM processes. The PMF can be used to assess individual processes, or the maturity of an organization's ITSM process as a whole.

> *An ITIL V3 Self Assessment Maturity Model is available as a*
> *subscription service at www.bestpracticelive.com. This model*
> *can be used to establish the maturity of your ITIL V3 processes.*

5.1 Getting Started

It is important to understand when you initiate an assessment that there is a difference between conducting an audit and assessing process maturity:

- An **audit** examines evidence to determine compliance with a law, regulation, policy, or standard
- An **assessment** is an evaluation undertaken to:
  - Baseline an organization's strengths and weaknesses
  - Identify and recommend process improvement opportunities, priorities, and next steps

Assessments can be conducted in a variety of informal and formal ways including:

- By a process owner
- By a process improvement team
- By an independent party such as an internal auditor or an external consultant

The approach selected will vary based on factors such as the type of organization (e.g., internal or external service provider), its size, and its goals.

An effective technique for conducting a process maturity assessment is to establish a **process improvement team (PIT)** that designs or redesigns a process and determines how best to implement the new process across the organization. Begin by having each member of the PIT independently complete a self-assessment questionnaire. A CPDE, project manager, or facilitator can then assemble the results and facilitate a consensus. This technique enables an understanding of the varying perspectives and perceptions that exist among stakeholders, and aims to improve, through understanding, stakeholder relations.

5.2 Assessing Incident Management Maturity

This chapter describes an exercise aimed at assessing—at a high level—the maturity of a critical ITSM process—incident management.

Note that while this exercise uses incident management as an example, the maturity characteristics, challenges, and transition steps to the next level of maturity are relatively common from one process to the next. Note also that this assessment technique can be used to baseline the maturity of processes, or to monitor the effectiveness of improvement activities.

The matrices that follow describe the high-level characteristics of the incident management process as it moves through each stage of maturity. These matrices are *loosely* based on the ITIL PMF, which addresses the five areas of: vision and steering, process, people, technology, and culture. These matrices do not represent the detailed, task-oriented characteristics you will find in the *ITIL V3 Self Assessment Maturity Model*. Rather, they are designed to provide a middle ground look at the general factors that determine process maturity. These factors include:

- Objective attainment and business alignment
- Cost effectiveness and funding
- Accountability and process compliance
- Procedural compliance
- Lifecycle management
- Use of technology
- Data capture and availability of information
- Knowledge capture
- Proactive activities

- Predictive activities
- Customer satisfaction

The following is discussed for each level of maturity:

- Characteristics
- Challenges
- Transition steps

Using the matrices, check off the high-level characteristics that best describe your current incident management practices. The areas in which the majority of your checkmarks fall will help determine your current maturity level.

5.2.1 Level 1 (Initial): Characteristics

Table 5.1 shows typical characteristics of the *initial* level of maturity.

5.2.2 Level 1 (Initial): Challenges and Transition Steps

Organizations at the *initial* level of maturity typically have some form of incident management activities occurring within the organization, however, these activities have not been formally recognized as a process. These activities are instead represented by characteristics such as:

- Unwritten ways of working, often referred to as **tribal knowledge**
- Disjointed or loosely strung together written procedures
- A management team that micro-manages activities because:
  - Roles and responsibilities are loosely defined
  - Little to no performance management data is captured
  - Few tools exist to drive work flow

Level 1 Challenges

Challenges to overcome at this level of maturity are many and include:

- Lack of commitment from management and staff
- Lack of understanding about business needs and required service levels
- Resistance to change as processes are perceived as bureaucratic

Level 1 Transition Steps

Transition steps at this level of maturity include:

- Gaining management commitment
- Allocating resources to process definition and design activities
- Adopting organizational change management best practices
  - Communicate, communicate, communicate

Table 5.1 Characteristics of the *initial* level of maturity

High-level incident management process maturity characteristics
Level 1 (initial):
• Objectives are unclear—little (if any) integration exists with service level management and reporting is nominal
• Costs are high (due to inefficiencies) and not fully understood—minimal funds are available for process design and improvement
• Incident ownership is unclear and is passed to those working on the incident—process roles and responsibilities are also unclear
• Procedures are informal at best—incidents are handled in a random fashion
• Recording, tracking, and status accounting activities are seen as taking too much time—such activities are viewed as getting in the way of work
• Few tools are being used—the tools that do exist were informally selected and implemented and the procedures for using the tool are seen as the "process"
• Little data is being captured and little information is available for continual improvement—what information is available is received as criticism
• Little (if any) knowledge is captured—little (if any) integration exists with processes such as configuration, knowledge, and release management
• Incident rediscovery is common and widespread—few efforts are made to capture solutions or determine root cause via problem management
• Few predictive activities are occurring (e.g., trend analysis, integration with change and release management, and integration with planning processes such as availability and capacity management)—incidents happen, people react
• Customer needs are ignored—satisfaction is low

> ***Organizational change management*** *is the process of preparing, motivating, and equipping people to meet new business challenges. Organizational change management is discussed in chapter 9.*

While it is common practice to do so, organizations at this stage lack the maturity needed to:

- Select and implement technology
- Implement service level agreements
- Reorganize

5.2.3 Level 2 (Repeatable): Characteristics

Table 5.2 shows typical characteristics at the *repeatable* level of maturity.

5.2.4 Level 2 (Repeatable): Challenges and Transition Steps

Organizations at the *repeatable* stage of maturity recognize the need to:

- Allocate resources to process definition activities
- Document and (re)design processes and procedures
- Capture and begin using data to improve performance

Table 5.2 Characteristics of the *repeatable* level of maturity

High-level incident management process maturity characteristics
Level 2 (repeatable):
• Objectives are still unclear—some integration may exist with service level management but metrics are just numbers
• Costs, particularly hidden costs, continue to be misunderstood—funds and resources are made available for process design and improvement
• Incident ownership is unclear and is passed to those working on the incident—roles and responsibilities are defined at a team or function level
• Some procedures have been defined but activities continue to be primarily reactive—people are focused on "fire fighting"
• Recording, tracking, and status accounting activities are erratic—data are captured when "time allows"
• Tools, some home grown, are being introduced in an ad hoc and stand alone manner—few controls are in place
• Data is being stored in a variety of locations and little information is available for continual improvement—what information is available is received as criticism
• Some knowledge is being captured at a team or function level—little (if any) integration exists with processes such as configuration, knowledge, and release management
• Incident rediscovery is common and widespread—some solutions are being captured; however, few efforts are being made to determine the root cause via integration with problem management
• Few predictive activities are occurring (e.g., trend analysis, integration with change management, and integration with planning processes such as availability and capacity management)—the culture remains primarily reactive
• Customer needs are made a priority—doing "whatever it takes" to satisfy the customer becomes the prevailing catchphrase without the structure of a formalized policy or process

Level 2 Challenges

Challenges to overcome at this level of maturity include figuring out:

- Where to start
- Who to involve
- How to find time

Another big challenge at this level of maturity is recognizing that IT cannot be "all things to all people." Catchphrases such as "whatever it takes," and "get 'er done," often backfire as people do whatever it takes to satisfy customers; even though "whatever" may not be in the organization's best interest. Care must be taken to ensure policies, processes, and procedures are clear and that people are required to follow them.

Level 2 Transition Steps

A good place to start with process definition activities is a best practice framework. Such frameworks offer guidance in terms of the purpose of each process, along with process goals and objectives, boundaries, suppliers, customers, and so forth. Using one or more best practice frameworks optimizes the benefits of industry research and avoids reinventing the wheel.

Documenting processes and procedures also may not involve starting from scratch. Rather, it typically involves documenting an "as is" process that:

- Has not been agreed upon by all of its stakeholders
- Has not previously been formally defined or documented
- Has never been assessed and aligned with best practice

Transition steps at this level of maturity include:

- Ensuring customer requirements are understood and prioritized
- Identifying applicable frameworks and benchmarking performance
- Defining, designing, and implementing the new process
- Baselining performance metrics where possible
- Stepping up organizational change management activities

Recall that benchmarking is the process of comparing an organization's practices and performance metrics to those of another organization, or to industry best practices and industry average metrics, in an effort to identify improvement opportunities. A **baseline** provides a starting point against which to measure the effect of process improvements. In the case of performance metrics, a baseline is a snapshot of performance metrics at a given point in time.

When implementing a new process or procedure, remember to communicate what *not* to do anymore, as well as what to do. Process assessments often reveal steps being taken or reports being produced that are no longer needed, but no one ever stated explicitly that they could be stopped. A common refrain is "it's just the way we've always done it."

5.2.5 Level 3 (Defined): Characteristics

Table 5.3 shows typical characteristics at the *defined* level of maturity.

5.2.6 Level 3 (Defined): Challenges and Transition Steps

Organizations at the *defined* level of maturity have:

- Recognized incident management as a process
- Designated a process owner
- Defined, designed, and implemented a new process
- Begun measuring performance against agreed targets
- Begun to see some of the benefits of a process-oriented culture

Level 3 Challenges

Management commitment and strong organizational change management are critical at this stage of maturity to overcome confusion about the new process and resistance to change. Culture change is difficult and without persistence at this stage of maturity, the organization can easily slip back into old behaviors.

It is also common for organizations to get stuck at this level of maturity, particularly when strong management commitment and organizational change management are lacking. This is because once the process has been defined, some basic tools have been implemented, and the staff has been trained, there is a temptation to think the work is done. Or, perhaps customer satisfaction has increased to the point where there are fewer customer complaints, and so management becomes confident that the organization is handling incidents efficiently and effectively.

Questions that must be considered include:

- Are the goals of incident management linked to business plans?
- Has incident management been accepted across the organization?
- Is incident management fully integrated with other ITSM processes?
- Is incident management integrated with external suppliers' processes?

Another common mistake that organizations make at this stage of maturity is to create process silos. With process silos, teams of people are dedicated to performing a single process, such as the release team, or the change team. People working in these teams may be quite focused and perform that single process well; but may fail to understand how it relates to other processes. Remember that a single process will never fully mature if it is not integrated with all of the other ITSM processes.

Table 5.3 Characteristics of the *defined* level of maturity

High-level incident management process maturity characteristics
Level 3 (defined):
• Objectives are understood—formal targets are being set via service level management and metrics are being used to measure performance
• Costs, particularly hidden costs, are starting to be understood—design and improvement activities are well funded and adequately resourced
• Incident ownership is clearly defined—roles and responsibilities are clearly defined and training plans are in place
• Incidents are being handled in accordance with business impact and urgency—priorities have been established
• Recording, tracking, and status accounting activities are recognized as valuable—data, information, and knowledge are being captured
• Integrated tools are being introduced in a controlled manner—workflow and reporting activities are increasingly being automated
• Data collection is being controlled and data sources are being consolidated; information is available for continuous improvement—data accuracy and completeness is sometimes called into question but is improving; the value of information is being recognized
• Some knowledge is being captured at an organizational level—some integration is occurring with processes such as configuration, knowledge, and release management
• Incident rediscovery is reduced—efforts are being made to capture solutions and workarounds, along with the root cause via integration with problem management; some incidents are being prevented
• Predictive activities are starting to occur via integration with processes such as change, release, availability, and capacity management—some incidents are anticipated
• Customer needs are recognized—satisfaction is increasing

Level 3 Transition Steps

Several key steps are needed at this level of maturity to capitalize on the progress made to date and continue to mature. Those steps include:

- Recognize the role of the service desk in successful incident management
- Ensure the tone of incident management reporting is positive
- Reduce the number of disparate, uncontrolled tools being used
- Ensure the incident management process and system are aligned
- Avoid over customizing the incident management system

Not all organizations need to achieve Level 4 and, ultimately, Level 5 maturity for all processes. The cost to do so may be too great. For some organizations, particularly smaller organizations, or for some processes, achieving Level 3 may demonstrate significant and sustainable improvement. Assessments must continue to be conducted and efforts must be taken to sustain Level 3, however, or it is likely that performance problems will arise.

While the focus is still on maturing the incident management process, notice that technology becomes much more important as an organization matures. This is because capturing accurate and complete data, and using that data to produce information and knowledge, are hallmarks of high performing organizations. Not just any data or information, but data and information that continually enable the organization to satisfy customer requirements.

5.2.7 Level 4 (Managed): Characteristics

Table 5.4 shows typical characteristics at the *managed* level of maturity.

5.2.8 Level 4 (Managed): Challenges and Transition Steps

Organizations at the *managed* level of maturity:

- Have implemented incident management across the organization
- Have established interfaces with other ITSM processes
- Are managing the process through the use of business-focused performance metrics

Level 4 Challenges

Leadership and vision are always important but are of vital importance at this level of maturity. The cultural challenges cannot be underestimated including:

- Failing to acknowledge customer complaints and changing customer requirements
- Ensuring management views process improvement as real work
- Recognizing the importance of ongoing communication, education, and training
  - New and transferred employees must receive formal process and tool-related training
  - Key employees should receive advanced education and training and participate in industry events

- Establishing appropriate interfaces with new processes and maintaining integration with existing processes as those processes are continually improved

Table 5.4 Characteristics of the *managed* level of maturity

High-level incident management process maturity characteristics
Level 4 (managed):
• Objectives are understood—formal targets are being set via service level management and metrics are being used to measure performance
• Costs, including hidden costs, are being managed—design and improvement activities are well funded and adequately resourced
• Incident ownership is clearly defined—roles and responsibilities are clearly defined and reflected in job descriptions
• Incidents are being handled in accordance with business impact and urgency—priorities are understood
• Recording, tracking, and status accounting activities are recognized as a requirement of the job—meaningful data, information, and knowledge are being captured
• Integrated tools are being used—workflow, reporting, and control activities are increasingly automated
• Data collection is being controlled and definitive data sources have been identified; information is available for continuous improvement—data accuracy and completeness are trusted
• Knowledge is increasingly being captured at an organizational level—integration is occurring with processes such as configuration and release management
• Incident rediscovery is minimized—solutions and workarounds are captured, along with the root cause via integration with problem management; incidents are being prevented
• Predictive activities are occurring via integration with processes such as change, release, availability, and capacity management—change-related incidents are anticipated
• Customer needs are recognized—customers are satisfied

Level 4 Transition Steps

Transition steps at this level of maturity are really tied to the overall maturity of the organization and its ability to recognize the importance of continual improvement, business and IT alignment, and process integration. Processes at this level of maturity must be monitored, measured, and continually improved, and it must be understood that no single process can mature beyond this stage on its own.

> *The best companies recognize the need for, or already have in place, a QMS that facilitates and enables continual process improvement.*

Relative to the incident management process, a QMS ensures that:

- Business impact drives the IT organization's efforts to prevent, prioritize, and resolve incidents
- All aspects of incident management—people, processes, technology, and information—have been considered and are integrated
- A team perspective prevails, facilitated by an integrated tool suite
- The incident management process is effectively integrated with other ITSM processes
- The incident management process is effectively integrated with external suppliers' processes

Key steps to sustain process efficiency and effectiveness at this level of maturity include:

- Continue to allocate resources—organizations are often tempted at this level of maturity to begin reallocating resources. For example, the individual responsible for implementing the incident management system is assigned to a new project. As a result, system maintenance is neglected, system performance starts to slow down, and upgrades are put on hold. Or, the incident management process owner leaves the company and management fails to fill that role. As a result, the process health metrics go unmonitored, and perhaps begin to decline with no one to notice. Although time commitments should go down as processes continue to mature, resources must be allocated to ongoing maintenance and continual improvement activities.
- Train new employees and managers—organizations often provide comprehensive training when a process and system is first released. New employees and managers must receive that same level of training. This does not imply that the fresh ideas these new employees may introduce should not be welcomed. Rather, it ensures new employees and managers understand the existing processes, and their related processes, before suggesting changes.
- Provide ongoing training to existing employees—strive to ensure process and system changes along with the benefits of those changes are communicated, even if only in the form of informal training classes or presentations.
- Solicit feedback when changes are made—ensure the benefits are understood and realized. Point out when changes are being made at the suggestion of customers and staff so that people know their ideas are valued.
- Conduct regular reviews and audits—ensure the cost, quality, efficiency, and effectiveness goals of the incident management process continue to be in sync with the needs of the business. Conduct regular audits to ensure compliance with process activities.

5.2.9 Level 5 (Optimizing): Characteristics

Note that this level of maturity is titled optimizing, versus optimized, in recognition that continual improvement efforts are still not done. Table 5.5 shows typical characteristics at the Optimizing level of maturity.

5.2.10 Level 5 (Optimizing): Challenges and Transition Steps

Organizations at the *optimizing* level of maturity:

- Continually improve the incident management process
- Have fully integrated incident management with other ITSM processes
- Have changed the culture of their organization from:
  - People dependent to process dependent
  - Reactive to proactive
  - Technology centric to business centric

Level 5 Challenges

This level of maturity is extremely difficult to sustain. Continual improvement becomes much more difficult, and can become costly. Leadership, vision, and management commitment are critical.

How can management demonstrate commitment? There are certain aspects of incident management that an organization must just accept. For example, there will always be that one vice president who feels compelled to bypass the service desk and contact an IT manager directly. Or, there will be technical specialists who cannot update incident records without putting up a fight. In these situations, management must demonstrate their commitment to the process through both words and deeds.

For example, the IT manager can ask the vice president if he or she has contacted the service desk and if not, indicate that "I can take care of this for you and will also ensure the service desk is notified." This approach tells the vice president that contacting the service desk is important and also provides the service desk the information it needs to be successful.

Management must clearly communicate incident management policy to the company's technical specialists and align that policy with the specialists' performance plan. For example, failure to record incidents could mean the specialist is not assigned to an exciting new project or receives a lower bonus. Management can also ensure that job candidates are aware that following the incident management process, documenting incidents, and sharing their expertise by contributing to a knowledgebase are job requirements.

Table 5.5 Characteristics of the *optimizing* level of maturity

High-level incident management process maturity characteristics
Level 5 (optimizing):
• Objectives are being met—service levels are continually monitored and improvement via the service level management process and continual improvement is a way of life
• Costs have been minimized—an accurate forecast of resource requirements can be provided
• Incident owners manage by exception—process compliance is high
• Incidents are being handled in accordance with business impact and urgency and within predefined targets—priorities are understood
• Recording, tracking, and status accounting activities are automated where possible—systems are managing systems, people are managing the business
• Integrated tools are being exploited—workflow, reporting, and control activities are automated where possible
• Data collection is automated where possible and definitive data sources are being controlled—data accuracy and completeness are high
• Knowledge is being captured at an organizational level—incident management is fully integrated with processes such as configuration, knowledge, and release management
• Incident rediscovery is minimized—incident management is fully integrated with problem management; incidents are being proactively prevented
• Predictive activities are occurring via integration with processes such as change, release, availability, and capacity management—change-related incidents are being minimized
• Customer self-sufficiency is enhanced—satisfaction is high

Level 5 Transition Steps

Key steps to sustain this level of maturity include:

- Understand the metrics lifecycle—the time may come when steady improvement can no longer occur without considerable cost. For example, first line resolution at the service desk may steadily increase initially, but in time will normalize, and may in time begin to decrease. This is because an effective problem management process will eliminate recurring incidents. As a result, the incidents being reported are unique and more complex, and so may require the expertise of higher levels of support. This causes a reduction in first line resolution at the service desk. This may also cause a longer incident resolution time. Management must consider how the activities of one process can influence the efficiency and effectiveness of another process and adjust accordingly. Failing to consider this lifecycle could result in low morale as people work hard, but cannot seem to achieve process goals and meet management's expectations. Or, unwanted behavior may occur as people try to find a way to be successful, even though the time has come to redefine success.

- Begin producing business-centric metrics—a key objective of the incident management process is to minimize business impact, but what does that mean? True alignment exists when IT is able to use business metrics to show how the IT organization contributes to the business' goals, rather than simply reporting operational performance. For example, rather than reporting 98.6 percent availability, use incident data to determine the amount of revenue lost as a result of unavailability, or the number of product sales that were lost because a system was down. Conversely, strive to demonstrate how a streamlined incident management process and incident data enables the IT organization to continually improve the quality of its services.

Incident management was used in this exercise but the PMF can be used to assess the maturity of any ITSM process. Periodically benchmarking existing processes against other organizations or a best practice framework is an excellent way to determine process improvement opportunities and continually improve processes.

Steps to take following an assessment include:

- Perform a gap analysis (discussed in Chapter 6)
- Initiate improvement projects with target dates and specific and measurable goals
- Schedule subsequent assessments at appropriate intervals, based on your organization's goals

The next section describes a methodical approach to designing and improving processes, including how to perform a gap analysis.

Summary

Organizations are rarely able to withstand the culture change required to move from having no process to having a high-performing process in a short period of time. It is also uncommon for organizations to have all of the components of a successful process—people, processes, technology, and information—in place and in a mature state when a process is first being designed and implemented. A far better approach is to recognize that organizations and processes mature over time.

A cornerstone of continual process improvement is assessing the current level of maturity and determining the steps that must be taken to move to the next maturity level. Models that can be used to assess process maturity include CMMI, ISO/IEC 15504, and the ITIL PMF.

Assessments can be conducted in a variety of informal and formal ways. The approach selected will vary based on factors such as the type of organization, its size, and its goals. Regardless of the approach selected, an effective technique for assessing process maturity is to establish a PIT comprised of all stakeholders. This technique enables an understanding of the varying perspectives and perceptions that exist among stakeholders, and aims to improve, through understanding, stakeholder relations.

Assessing process maturity involves comparing the characteristics or activities of your current process, to those of a mature process. Such an effort also involves identifying the challenges that must be overcome, and the transition steps that must be taken, to move to the next level of maturity.

Discussion Topics

- A common perception is that once a process is implemented, the work is "done." What are the ramifications of such a perception?
- Establishing a baseline is an important starting point when benchmarking a process. How are baselines used and why are they important?
- A single process will never fully mature if it is not integrated with other processes. Why is process integration so important?

Review Questions

1. Briefly explain the difference between continual and continuous process improvement.
2. Briefly discuss the difference between an audit and an assessment.
3. List and briefly describe the five stages of process maturity in the ITIL PMF.
4. What are two challenges commonly found at the *initial* level of maturity?
5. In which stage of process maturity is an "as is" process documented?
6. Why is it common for organizations to get stuck at the *defined* level of maturity?
7. True or false. The goal of most organizations is to achieve at least a level 4 maturity. Explain your answer.
8. List four key steps to sustain process efficiency and effectiveness at the *managed* level of maturity.
9. Define and give an example of business-centric metrics.
10. What three steps should be taken following a maturity assessment?

6

Process Design and Improvement Steps

The prospect of creating a comprehensive process definition document such as the one in appendix A may intimidate you. Keep in mind, however, that a well-designed and documented process provides the ability to:

- Identify needed changes to job descriptions, employee performance management programs, and incentive programs (people)
- Develop and document the procedures that employees and external suppliers or partners need to do their work (processes)
- Identify tool requirements (technology)
- Determine the data to collect and the reports to prepare in order to measure process performance (information)
- Document the vocabulary to use when promoting, performing, and discussing a process (marketing/awareness)

It is also important to understand that the absence of a well-designed and documented process is a characteristic of the *initial* level of maturity. Designing and documenting a process enables an organization to begin making the transition from the *initial* (ad hoc or chaotic) level of maturity, through the *repeatable* level, to the *defined* level.

The **ten process design and improvement steps**, illustrated in Figure 6.1, provide a sound methodology that can be used to design and improve any process regardless of maturity level. These steps are iterative in nature and so can help move an organization from one level of maturity to the next.

This methodology provides the common vocabulary, tools, and techniques needed to get all stakeholders involved in process design and improvement activities. Once involved, using this methodical approach helps to keep all stakeholders

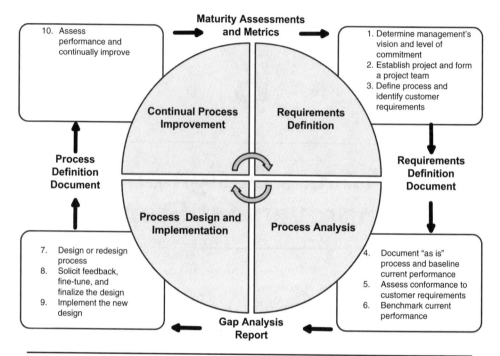

Figure 6.1   Ten process design and improvement steps

going in the same direction and focused on achieving the same goals—efficient and effective processes that satisfy your customers' requirements.

The ten process design and improvement steps are grouped into four logical phases. Figure 6.1 shows that each phase produces a deliverable that serves as input to the next phase. These phases, deliverables, and steps include:

Requirements Definition—Requirements Definition Document

1. Determine management's vision and level of commitment
2. Establish project and form a project team
3. Define process and identify customer requirements

Process Analysis—Gap Analysis Report

4. Document "as is" process and baseline current performance
5. Assess conformance to customer requirements
6. Benchmark current performance

Process Design and Implementation—Process Definition Document

7. Design or redesign process

8. Solicit feedback, fine-tune, and finalize the design
9. Implement the new design

Continual Process Improvement—Maturity Assessments and Metrics

10. Assess performance and continually improve

The ten steps help to:

- Define and understand an end-to-end process, its customers, their requirements, and the process components that enable those requirements to be met
- Keep a process current within your organizational structure, related processes, and available technologies
- Continually assess and improve a process

A CPDE may oversee the execution of the ten step methodology and/or may serve in multiple roles including:

- Project manager
- Facilitator
- Process analyst
- Process design engineer
- Process owner
- Process manager

The following provides a detailed description of each step.

6.1 Step 1: Determine Management's Vision and Level of Commitment

Determining management's vision and level of commitment is a critical first step for a number of reasons.

First, it's important to ask management, particularly senior management, what they want the process design effort to accomplish. In other words, what is their vision? Design efforts can focus on all or any number of process characteristics including cost, quality, efficiency, effectiveness, customer satisfaction, and employee satisfaction. Design efforts may also focus on adopting best practices or achieving compliance with a standard such as ISO/IEC 20000. Ask management to quantify the improvements desired to the extent possible. This insight will serve as input to the baselining and benchmarking activities that follow.

Secondly, management's commitment in terms of resource allocation must be determined at this time as it will considerably influence the scope of the project. If limited resources are available, it is better to limit the scope of the project and achieve continual improvement through a series of "baby" steps. It is also important from an organizational change management perspective. Mistrust and dissatisfaction will result if you promise more than can be delivered given available resources.

Lastly, it is important to discuss with management—early on—factors such as:

- Priorities
- Project risks
- Barriers to process improvement
- Employee fears
- How management can demonstrate commitment

These factors will continue to be discussed as the project scope is defined and the project plan is developed.

6.2 Step 2: Establish a Project and Form a Project Team

IT organizations are notoriously lax when it comes to treating internal process design and improvement activities as a project. As a result, critical components of effective project management such as communication and organizational change management are often neglected.

Establish a Project

Establishing a project begins with an initiation phase during which a project idea is linked to the strategic goals and objectives of the organization and formally authorized. A **project charter** is a short document that formally authorizes the project and empowers the project manager.

Once a project is charted, project planning can begin. Project planning involves describing in detail the work to be done, how and when the work will be done, and by whom. Planning also includes defining the project scope in greater detail. The project scope of a process design and improvement project will vary based on factors such as:

- Whether your organization is new to process design
- Whether you are designing a new process or simply improving an existing process
- Whether you are focusing on a single process or multiple integrated processes
- The maturity of processes that interface with the process(es) being (re) designed
- The influence the project team will have over interfacing processes

The results of a process maturity assessment provide excellent input to the project scoping decision.

To avoid project scope creep, it is critical that clear boundaries be defined in terms of project goals and objectives, and most importantly, the business needs driving the project. A **project scope statement** describes in detail the work to be done and serves as an agreement between all stakeholders of the project. A project scope statement typically includes:

- Project goals and objectives
- Project boundaries (in scope and out of scope)
- Associated legal and regulatory controls
- Project deliverables
- Acceptance criteria to be met before the deliverables are accepted
- Considerations and concerns

In the case of small projects, the project scope statement may be submitted as a request for change (RFC) and approved via your company's change management process. For larger projects, a business case may be required to justify the initiation of a project. A **business case** is a report that describes the business reasons that a change is being considered, along with its associated costs, benefits, and risks. Chapter 7 describes producing a business case in greater detail.

Regardless of project size, it is important to identify a project sponsor who will approve the final project scope. The **project sponsor** has ultimate authority over the project and secures project funding. The project sponsor also:

- Provides high-level guidance to the project team
- Resolves issues when necessary
- Approves scope changes
- Approves major deliverables

In other words, the project sponsor is responsible for ensuring the project is aligned with business needs, customer requirements, and current business and IT policies, such as spending policies.

> *A project sponsor is typically an individual in a leadership position who has the authority and commitment to change how the organization operates.*

In the case of larger projects, the project sponsor may oversee a management planning committee. Members of a **management planning committee** participate in high-level goal and scope setting activities. Members of this committee must possess a clear understanding of the project objectives, have a vested interest in the success of the project, have the authority to make decisions relative to the activities in which they are involved, and must possess a willingness to discuss their opinions and participate in the reaching of a consensus.

In some organizations, larger projects may also be reviewed by an IT strategy or steering group. ITIL views the **IT steering group (ISG)** as a formal group of senior representatives from both the business and IT who are responsible for ensuring that business and IT strategies and plans are closely aligned. ISG activities include:

- Reviewing policies and the IT organization's portfolio of services
- Authorizing and prioritizing projects
- Ensuring realistic implementation timescales
- Reviewing projects to ensure the business benefits are being realized

Day-to-day project activities are the responsibility of the project manager and so care must be taken to ensure the skills of the project manager are a right fit for the project scope. The **project manager** leads the project team and is assigned the authority and responsibility for overseeing the project and meeting the project's objectives.

The project manager also maintains the **project plan**, which is a set of documents that describe a project, its objectives, and how the objectives are to be achieved. The project plan includes:

- Purpose, goals, and objectives
- Background
- Scope
- Deliverables
- Assumptions and constraints
- Related projects and critical dependencies
- Schedule and milestones
- Budget and cost-benefit assessment
- Risk assessment
- Work breakdown structure
- Quality management approach
- Tools and techniques
- Resource estimates
- Standards
- Project change control procedures
- Roles and responsibilities
- Work plan
- Team contact directory
- Approval sign-off form

Form a Project Team

Depending on the scope of the project, the project manager may oversee a project team comprised of one or more committees, sub-teams, or project resources. Examples include:

- Process improvement team
- Software selection committee
- Software design team
- Technical writer
- Facilitator

Resources associated with your company's change, release, configuration, and knowledge management processes (just to name a few) will also be engaged.

As our focus is on process design and improvement, the most important team to discuss is the process improvement team (PIT). The PIT designs or redesigns a process and determines how best to implement the new process across the organization. The PIT includes all process stakeholders; that is, any person or group who is or might be affected by changes to the process. Stakeholders in a process design or improvement project may include: the project sponsor, business customers, users, IT management, IT staff, suppliers, and change agents. A **change agent** helps people move towards change. Change agents are discussed in greater detail in Chapter 9.

More specifically, stakeholders are people or groups who may be:

- Responsible for process activities
- Accountable for process activities
- Consulted about process activities
- Informed about process activities

A **RACI matrix**—also known as an **ARCI matrix**—maps roles and responsibilities to the activities of a process. A RACI matrix can also be used to map the roles and responsibilities of the people and teams engaged in a project with project tasks. Chapter 7 describes creating and using a RACI matrix in greater detail.

> *Stakeholders can have a positive or negative impact on project and process design activities and so must be actively engaged.*

For process design and implementation activities to be successful, all stakeholders must be engaged to ensure:

- Their perceptions, needs, and expectations are understood and considered
- Their knowledge and experience is utilized
- Their cooperation and buy-in are obtained
- Process design efforts are viewed as credible

Without stakeholder involvement and support, it is highly likely that process design and improvement efforts may be ignored, criticized, resisted, or sabotaged.

PIT responsibilities include understanding:

- How the current process is working (good, bad, and ugly)

- How stakeholders, and most importantly, customers would like the process to work
- The organization's ability to absorb change
- Needed process controls and measures

Chapter 8 discusses process controls and measures in greater detail.

Two of the most important roles are the process owner and the process manager. Optimally, the individuals filling these roles are identified in advance and are able to participate in process design activities.

A **process owner** is accountable for overall process quality and ensures conformance to the process. Process owners are typically senior managers who have the authority to define process policies, strategies, critical success factors (CSFs), key performance indicators (KPIs), and metrics.

A process owner also works with line managers to ensure that sufficient resources are allocated to process activities and that the staff receives adequate training.

A **process manager** is responsible for operational (day-to-day) management of a process. While specific responsibilities will vary from one process to the next, process manager responsibilities generally consist of:

- Ensuring the successful end-to-end execution of the process
- Identifying issues and exceptions for the process owner
- Acting as a focal point for the process
- Communicating with process suppliers, customers, and management
- Ensuring management reports are prepared and analyzed
- Monitoring KPIs and process metrics and alerting the process owner and management when goals are not being met
- Chairing or participating in process reviews and audits
- Formulating and executing improvement action plans

> *In smaller organizations, the process owner and process manager roles may be combined.*

Other committees and resources may form part of the greater project team. Members of the PIT may participate on these committees or other people may be engaged.

> *When new people are brought into the project team or new committees are formed, care must be taken to ensure the project goals and previously made decisions are clearly communicated and understood. A strong project manager helps avoid unnecessary or inappropriate backward steps that may be caused by an influx of new viewpoints.*

Other project committees and resources may include:

- **Software selection committee**—members of this committee will identify system requirements following process design. The team will then identify and evaluate systems that conform to those requirements and make a final recommendation to management. Team members must possess a clear understanding of the end-to-end process and of the defined requirements, along with a willingness to select a system that meets the needs of the entire organization.
- **Software design committee**—members of this team will participate in the definition of screen layouts, menus, reports, etc., as needed to configure and customize the selected system to the process. Team members must possess a willingness to obtain an understanding of the capabilities of the selected tool, a clear understanding of the process(es) the tool will support, and the analytical ability required to create screen layouts, menus, reports, and so forth that are intuitive, logical, and user friendly.
- **Technical writer**—this resource assists with the creation of required documents, procedures, and training materials. The technical writer takes direction from the project manager.
- **Facilitator**—this critical person serves as a project resource and leads the PIT through the process design and improvement steps.

Quick Tip: The Facilitator's Role	It has been said that the facilitator's responsibility is to focus on the journey, rather than the destination. Care must be taken when selecting a facilitator for process definition and design activities. This resource should be knowledgeable about quality improvement methods and techniques such as mapping processes, baselining performance, using best practices, facilitating meetings, and building teams. The role of the facilitator is to remain neutral while guiding the team to a decision. The most effective facilitators serve as an educator or team coach, rather than as an expert with all of the answers. An ineffective facilitator who asserts his or her opinion on the team can damage team dynamics and, ultimately, undermine the team's success. Some organizations hire a consultant to serve as a facilitator in an effort to ensure neutrality and bring to the project a skilled resource. Being an effective facilitator is a learned skill and so organizations may also strive to develop and maintain this skill in house.

As mentioned previously, the project scope determines the teams, committees, and resources needed to design and implement a new or improved process.

In the event that multiple processes are being addressed within the scope of a single project, the stakeholders and resources involved will vary accordingly, and the steps that follow will be applied to each process.

A critical step before proceeding is to hold a project kickoff meeting. During the project kickoff meeting, the facilitator, the project manager, and the process owner:

- Honor what has been done well in the past
- Describe the current situation and the need for change
    - Describe the cost of doing nothing
    - Create a sense of urgency
- Discuss the project scope, goals, and objectives
    - Create a vision of the future
    - Reinforce the vision set forth by senior management
- Empower team members to serve as change agents
- Establish team ground rules

Team ground rules are the rules a team agrees to live by to facilitate teamwork. Team ground rules include:

- Everyone is treated with respect
- Everyone is expected to keep an open mind
- Everyone is expected to keep the project scope, goals, and objectives in mind; no hidden agendas
- Everyone on the team is given a chance to speak
- Everyone's vote is equal
- There is no such thing as a dumb question or suggestion
- All feedback is considered and viewed as constructive
- Everyone shares the workload
- Individual and team accomplishments are recognized and celebrated
- The focus is on process issues; people issues are handled offline
- Decisions are made by consensus

A **consensus** is an opinion or position reached by all of a team's members or by a majority of its members. Reaching a consensus does not mean that team members take a vote and the majority rules, or that team members agree with the majority just to avoid conflict or move on to the next topic. A consensus is reached when all team members can say that either they agree with a decision, or they at least feel their point of view on a matter has been heard and understood, even if it has not been accepted. Once a consensus is reached, some team members may "agree to disagree" with the decision, but must still be willing to work toward its success.

6.3 Step 3: Define the Process and Identify Customer Requirements

A first step for the PIT is to define the process and establish measures.

Define the Process

Defining (versus designing) a process involves determining, at a high level, the process boundaries, interfaces, and how the process operates. Process definition activities include determining the process:

- Purpose, goals, and objectives
- Policies
- Triggers
- Boundaries including:
    o When the process starts
    o When the process ends
- Inputs and input suppliers
- Outputs and output customers

Effective process maps to produce at this stage in the process design and improvement lifecycle include a high-level integration map, or a relationship map. A **high-level integration** map shows the relationships that exist between interfacing processes. A **relationship** map depicts the supplier and customer relationships that exist within the boundaries of a process, across the major functions of the business. High-level integration and relationship maps are described in greater detail in Chapter 7.

This initial activity is critical as it enables the team to:

1. Further clarify the scope of the project
2. Verify that all stakeholders are engaged before detailed process design activities proceed

Identify Customer Requirements

Customer requirements are the driving force directing process design and improvement efforts.

Identifying customer requirements involves understanding how process customers are using process outputs, along with their expectations regarding output characteristics such as:

- Cost
- Quality
- Efficiency
- Effectiveness

Inputs to this step include the results of:

- Customer satisfaction surveys
- Annual needs assessments
- SLA performance metrics
- Benchmarking

Given sufficient resources, the ultimate goal is to satisfy *all* customer requirements. If it is not possible to satisfy all customer requirements immediately, work with customers to rank their needs in order of importance. If a process has multiple customer communities, develop a single, ranked list of requirements.

It is particularly important to identify legislative and regulatory requirements as those must be translated into process controls. A **control** is a rule designed to ensure that an organization is operating in a manner that adheres to corporate policies and procedures. The term control is most often used in the context of governance. According to the IT Governance Institute, **IT governance** is an integral part of enterprise governance and consists of the leadership and organizational structures and processes that ensure that the organization's information technology sustains and extends the organization's strategies and objectives. **Enterprise governance** is a set of responsibilities and practices exercised by an organization's board and executive management team with the goal of providing strategic direction, ensuring that objectives are achieved, ascertaining that risks are managed appropriately, and verifying that the enterprise's resources are used responsibly. Enterprise governance includes corporate governance which ensures compliance with laws such as the Sarbanes-Oxley Act of 2002 (SOX) and considers the welfare of shareholders.

Optimally, required controls are identified before process design begins. This ensures the evidence needed to satisfy the control is produced through the normal execution of the process. This is also important because adopting controls after a process is designed invariably causes the process to be cumbersome and is typically perceived as bureaucracy. Process controls are discussed in greater detail later in this chapter.

> *Once customer requirements are understood, supplier requirements must also be defined and documented as they will influence the ability of the process to produce the desired outcome.*

At this stage in the process design and improvement lifecycle, it should be possible for the PIT to document the "as is" process (if one exists) and begin establishing measures that can be used to baseline performance.

6.4 Step 4: Document the "As Is" Process and Baseline Current Performance

While there may be times that an organization begins designing a process "from scratch," it is far more common for an organization to have, even if only in an ad hoc form, some semblance of a process in place.

Document the "As Is" Process

Documenting the "as is" process is a critical step as it provides the PIT the ability to determine:

- What components of the process are working well
- What components of the process are not working well

> *Process components include people, the process itself and associated procedures, technology, and the information being used and produced by the process.*

An effective process map to produce at this stage in the process design and improvement lifecycle is a flowchart. Documenting the "as is" process also includes documenting process inputs, outputs, suppliers, customers, and so forth.

A common mistake is to skip the documenting of the "as is" process in an effort to quickly move on to process design activities. Doing so, however, often means the PIT lacks a full understanding of the work that people are actually doing. For example, people may be producing an input, or perhaps an output such as a report, because "that's the way they've always done it," even though the task is no longer required. Or, people may be doing work that they do not even realize is an activity within the boundaries of the process being (re)designed.

Producing an "as is" process involves:

- Talking with people who do the work to understand their activities and frustrations
- Identifying all of the deliverables such as documents, reports, or information being produced throughout the process
- Assessing the quality of deliverables
- Identifying all of the handoffs occurring throughout the process

A **handoff** occurs when a deliverable is passed from one person or function to another. Every handoff is an opportunity for error and so must be understood.

Baseline Current Performance

Another important step at this stage is to gather available measurable data that can be used to baseline current performance. Capturing a baseline at this stage of the process design and improvement lifecycle is critical as it can then be used later to demonstrate a return on investment. **Return on investment (ROI)** measures the quantifiable benefit derived from an investment and compares it with the total cost of the project. Benefits are typically tangible, such as reduced costs or increased profits. Determining the benefits derived from a project—such as a process improvement project—typically involves comparing a baseline or starting point with measures produced following an agreed period of time.

Measurable data that may be used to baseline performance includes:

- Error rates per activity
- Processing time per activity
- Rework activity

ROI is a subset of value on investment. **Value on investment (VOI)** is a measurement of the expected benefit of an investment. It represents both the financial (tangible) and non-monetary (intangible) value created by an investment. Examples include improved collaboration between the business and IT, improved ability to respond quickly to changing business conditions, and increased customer and employee satisfaction. Although VOI is subjective and more difficult to measure precisely than ROI, it is a valid and important part of the business case for change.

Two additional concepts that are often used in relation to process improvement initiatives are "quick win" and "proof of concept." A **quick win** is a result achieved within a short period of time with relatively little effort. Quick wins enable increased buy-in and momentum. **Proof of concept** is evidence that an idea or concept is feasible. Both of these milestones require that a baseline is captured for use as evidence that a desired result, or partial result, has been achieved.

While measures are important, they alone cannot be used to determine the effectiveness of an "as is" process. It is only when that process is compared to your customers' requirements that you can really begin to know how well a process is working.

In the absence of an "as is" process (e.g., in the event a completely new process is being introduced), an effective technique is to use a best practice process as a starting point, and compare that process to your customers' requirements. The process can also be defined from scratch, a technique often referred to as a "clean sheet" design. However, a clean sheet design is typically far more time consuming than using best practices and may result in reinventing the wheel.

6.5 Step 5: Assess Conformance to Customer Requirements

This step, and the next—benchmark current performance—both involve gap analysis. **Gap analysis** is a technique that determines the steps to be taken to move from a current state to a desired future state. Gaps can be determined using techniques such as:

- Analyzing requirements captured in a requirements definition document as a result of activities such as:
  - Surveying customers
  - Conducting an annual needs assessment
  - Creating and using SLAs
  - Benchmarking
- Analyzing balanced scorecards (discussed further in Chapter 8) to determine areas where customer needs are not being met

- Analyzing control charts to determine where abnormal performance variations exist (discussed further in Chapter 7)
- Analyzing customer complaints, compliments, and suggestions
- Analyzing the frustrations of people doing the work
- Producing an Ishikawa or cause-and-effect diagram to determine the causes of poor quality (discussed further in Chapter 7)

Gap analysis provides insight into areas where there is room for improvement. Identified gaps are assessed to determine factors such as:

- How frequently do quality problems occur?
- What is causing the gap?
- What steps can be taken to close the gap?
- Are improvement efforts justified in terms of time and cost savings?
- What measures can be used to know the gap has been closed?

Conclusions are captured in a **gap analysis report**, which is a formal document that summarizes the findings of a gap analysis.

6.6 Step 6: Benchmark Current Performance

Benchmarking is a powerful tool as it exposes organizations to innovative ideas, new ways of working, and best practices. Benchmarking can also soften the resistance of naysayers as they are able to see that a new idea is working successfully in another company.

Benchmarking may involve comparing your organization with:

- Competitors
- Best-in-class companies in your industry
- World-class companies regardless of industry
- Industry best practices
- Legal or regulatory requirements

The term **best-in-class** describes a company that has achieved the highest current level of performance in a particular industry. The term **world-class** describes a company that has achieved and is able to sustain high levels of customer satisfaction.

Companies benefit most from benchmarking when they identify opportunities for improvement, rather than simply comparing metrics. In other words, they uncover practices that can be used to eliminate quality problems and improve performance. Benchmarking against other companies involves:

- Identifying problem areas
- Identifying best-in-class or world-class companies that have similar processes
- Surveying or visiting high-performing organizations to identify alternative practices

- Generating ideas that can be used to address problem areas and satisfy customer requirements

Some companies are quite willing to discuss their practices and share information. In those cases, a site visit is an effective way to glean best practices. Other companies are unwilling to talk openly about their practices, but may be willing to participate in blind surveys where their identity is masked.

> *Companies such as Gartner (www.gartner.com), Aberdeen Group (www.aberdeen.com), and Forrester Research (www.forrester.com) offer service management-related research and benchmarking services that can be used to compare performance and identify best practices in a confidential manner.*

Benchmarking may also involve comparing your organization to industry best practices or to legal and regulatory controls. Here is where frameworks and standards such as ITIL, COBIT, MOF, and ISO/IEC 20000 can also be used to close gaps and increase performance.

Conclusions from Steps 4, 5 and 6 are captured in a gap analysis report that serves as input to process design activities.

6.7 Step 7: Design or Redesign Process

The goal of this step is to create a process that achieves the desired outcomes in a manner that satisfies customers.

A common mistake that organizations make is to try and design the "perfect" process. Such a quest invariably takes too long and is, in the end, difficult to implement or sustain.

When approaching a process design or redesign, factors such as management's vision, time, effort, cost, organizational maturity, and organizational priorities must all be considered. A skilled facilitator and strong project manager will keep these factors in the forefront as process design activities proceed.

The most efficient approach to process design is to conduct one or more process design workshops. A workshop is the most efficient approach because all stakeholders are engaged at the same time in making decisions.

In a **process design workshop**, PIT members are led by a facilitator through a series of exercises aimed at designing or redesigning a process.

Workshop exercises include but are not limited to:

- Validate (from Step 3) the process:
  - Purpose, goals, and objectives
  - Policies
  - Boundaries

- o Inputs and suppliers
- o Outputs and customers
- Design or redesign the flow of activities within the boundaries of the process
- Define roles and responsibilities
- Define CSFs and KPIs (discussed in Chapter 8)
- Define high-level:
  - o Process controls
  - o Data requirements
  - o Reporting requirements
  - o Meeting requirements such as change advisory board meetings, post-implementation review meetings, or service review meetings
  - o Training requirements
  - o Review and audit requirements
  - o Communication and marketing plans

During the process design workshop, team members have available to them documents created during earlier activities such as the:

- Requirements definition document
- "As is" process
- Gap analysis report

An alternative approach is to provide a **process design workbook** that provides a brief assessment of the current environment and a summary of all decisions made to date. Publishing the process design workbook in advance of the workshop provides stakeholders the opportunity to discuss the decisions to be made with management and co-workers, and to fully prepare for the workshop.

Care must be taken when selecting workshop participants. Key characteristics include:

- Decision-making authority
- A willingness to:
  - o Listen
  - o Participate
  - o Contribute constructive ideas
  - o Focus on process-related issues (versus people issues)
  - o Be open minded
  - o Work towards consensus

It is also important to communicate that workshop objectives include:

- Providing senior management the information needed to act on recommendations and approve the new process
- Designing a process that:

- o Satisfies customer requirements
- o Achieves management's vision
- Clarifying and improving the relationships that exist between people and functions involved in executing the process
- Bringing about a standardized approach to executing the process
- Determining how best to implement and promote awareness of the process within IT and the business

During the workshop it is the facilitator's responsibility to:

1. Conduct the exercises
2. Facilitate decisions
3. Capture and record decisions
4. Keep the discussion on track and progressing

Flowcharts and cross-functional maps are effective process mapping techniques that can be used at this stage. A **cross-functional map** illustrates the flow of process activities across the major functions of an organization.

These techniques are time consuming and so the skill of the facilitator will determine how these techniques will be used during the workshop. A common practice is to use white boards, flip charts, and Post-it notes during the workshop, and then using flowcharting tools to record the results. (Process mapping and flowcharting tools are discussed in greater detail in Chapter 7.)

Quick Tip:	There will invariably be topics that cannot be resolved by the workshop participants either because they lack the information, time, or authority to develop a solution. Create a "parking lot" flip chart that can be used to record these topics. Listing topics in a parking lot enables stakeholders to move on to a new topic as they know that they have been heard. This technique also ensures that the topic is not forgotten and that future action is taken.

Quick Tip:	Use role-playing exercises to simulate and fine-tune the process. Walk through the end-to-end process and discuss handoffs and deliverables to ensure understanding. Bring the proposed process to life!

Simply put, process design uses (1) all of the information previously collected and (2) the insight and experience of process stakeholders (led by a skilled facilitator) to determine:

- What to design *out* of the existing process
- What to design *in* to the new process

Determining What to Design Out

If your "as is" process is accurate and complete and your gap analysis has been thorough, there are likely some obvious opportunities for process improvement such as:

- Reducing handoffs
- Eliminating bottlenecks
- Eliminating unnecessary checks and reviews
- Eliminating or correcting activities that result in rework
- Eliminating duplicate activities
- Capturing information once at the source
- Substituting parallel activities for sequential activities when possible
- Consolidating roles when possible

Determining What to Design In

Determining what to design in begins with an understanding of your customers' requirements. Stakeholders can then study the "as is" process and determine what value-adding activities are needed to meet those requirements, along with how those activities can be performed in the most efficient and effective way.

If new work is being created, the next decision is to determine where that work will be performed. This is easier said than done as "turf wars" can ensue; however, it is critical at this stage that common sense prevails. If possible, try not to be constrained by current job titles and organizational structures. If that is not an option, strive to achieve proven best practices such as:

- Providing a single point of contact for customers
- Pushing decision making down to the lowest level possible without losing accountability
- Ensuring work is performed where it makes the most sense
- Building quality in to the process through adequate and appropriate process controls

The end result of process design activities is a draft process definition document. This draft document is used to solicit and obtain the feedback needed to fine-tune and finalize the design.

Did you notice that automation wasn't discussed during this step? There is an old expression, "if you're doing things wrong and you automate them, you'll do them wrong faster." The PIT must first envision the new process and then begin looking for ways technology can support and further enhance the execution of the process. Keep in mind, however, that many of the available service management tools reflect, in varying degrees, existing best practices. Adopting a best practice framework, along with a tool set and vendor that is aligned with that framework, will significantly reduce the time spent on process design activities. In other words, don't reinvent the wheel!

6.8 Step 8: Solicit Feedback, Fine-tune, and Finalize the Design

In this step you submit the newly designed process to management and senior management (including, where appropriate, customer management) for their review and approval.

Keys to success at this stage of the process design and improvement lifecycle include:

- Setting a firm date for feedback
- Ensuring all questions and suggestions are captured
- Ensuring all considerations and concerns are addressed

The PIT may need to reconvene to resolve any issues or concerns before publishing a final document. Version control is critical to ensure all final decisions are reflected. A sample document control sheet is provided in Appendix B.

6.9 Step 9: Implement the New Process

Implement the new process . . . four little words that involve considerable effort and always take more time and money than you think they will. The change and release management policies of your company will certainly be a factor at this stage. The availability of resources to participate in the implementation effort, including external suppliers, must also be considered.

As discussed previously, additional committees and teams may be formed to perform tasks such as:

- Revising job descriptions (as needed) and developing and delivering training (people)
- Developing related procedures and work instructions (processes)
- Selecting, designing, developing, testing, and implementing related tools (technology)
- Producing measurement systems, metrics, and reports (information)

Project activities that must also be considered include:

- Developing a release and deployment plan
- Converting (if desired) existing data
- Conducting a pilot
  - Is a phased approach possible?
  - Is a complete "big bang" deployment the best approach?
- Determining what to do if something goes wrong

Appendix C provides a high-level implementation plan that reflects the many steps that comprise those four little words, ". . . implement the new process."

6.10 Step 10: Assess Performance and Continually Improve

This last step is actually one of the most difficult but is a hallmark of high-performing organizations. The best organizations understand:

- Processes are never done
- Customer requirements can change over time
- Old habits are hard to break and, unobserved, people will tend to fall back on old ways of working
- Processes are never perfect, particularly when first implemented
- There is always room for improvement

The remainder of this book is devoted to methods and techniques that can be used to continually improve your processes including:

- Using quality management tools and techniques
- Producing and using meaningful metrics
- Managing organizational change
- Evaluating, selecting, and implementing technology

Summary

A well-designed and documented process provides the ability to identify and address the people, process, technology, information, and marketing/awareness aspects of a process-related change. It is also required to make the transition from the *initial* (ad hoc or chaotic) level of maturity, through the *repeatable* and *defined* levels, to the *managed* level.

The ten process design and improvement steps provide a sound methodology that can be used to design and improve any process. These steps are iterative in nature and so can also be used to improve any process in an effort to move an organization from one level of maturity to the next.

This methodology provides the common vocabulary, tools, and techniques needed to get all stakeholders involved in process design and improvement activities. Once involved, using this methodical approach helps keep all stakeholders going in the same direction and focused on achieving the same goals—efficient and effective processes that satisfy your customers' requirements.

The ten process design and improvement steps are grouped into four logical phases, each of which produces a deliverable. The requirements definition phase involves determining management's vision and level of commitment, engaging all stakeholders and establishing a project, defining the process, and identifying customer requirements. The deliverable is a requirements definition document.

The process analysis phase produces a gap analysis report that maps the differences between the specified customer requirements and the "as is" process.

Gap analysis provides insight into areas where there is room for improvement. A baseline is also captured at this stage that can be used later to demonstrate a return on investment.

The process design and implementation phase produces a process definition document that provides a record of decisions made during the process design activities, along with a high-level implementation plan. This document is used to solicit feedback and fine-tune and finalize the design. It is also used to perform many of the activities involved in implementing the new design.

The continual process improvement phase is the most difficult but is a hallmark of high-performing organizations. This phase involves continually assessing process maturity and using meaningful metrics to improve performance. The best organizations understand that processes are never done and there is always room for improvement.

Discussion Topics

- Management commitment to process design, improvement, and implementation activities is critical. How can management demonstrate its commitment?
- A common reason that people resist processes is bureaucracy. What causes bureaucracy and how can it be prevented?
- There is often a temptation to begin with a tool and let it drive process design. What are the dangers in taking such an approach?

Review Questions

1. Why is determining management's vision and level of commitment a critical first step when designing or improving a process?
2. How can you avoid "scope creep" in a process design project?
3. Who has ultimate authority over a project and secures project funding?
4. What is the difference between a process owner and a process manager?
5. Documenting the "as is" process provides you with the ability to determine what two things?
6. Why is it critical to baseline current performance in step 4 when redesigning a process?
7. What is gap analysis?
8. How can companies benefit most from benchmarking?
9. Why is a process design workshop an efficient approach to process design?
10. Provide four examples of items that you might design out of an existing process.

7

Process Design and Improvement Tools and Techniques

A variety of proven tools and techniques can be used to document, design and continually improve processes. The effective use of these tools and techniques requires:

- People skilled in their use
- Involvement by the people who perform the processes
- The commitment of management to continual improvement

These tools and techniques include:

- Process maps
- The seven basic tools of quality
- Business cases
- Return on investment calculations
- RACI matrices

7.1 Process Maps

Process mapping, also known as process charting and flowcharting, is a highly effective technique for making work visible. Process maps show the sequence of tasks that occur within a process, and also the relationship one process has with other processes. They provide a visual representation for people working on processes in the course of process design and improvement, or for people working within processes.

Process maps can assume several forms including:

- High-level integration maps
- Relationship maps; also known as SIPOC (supplier, input, process, output, and customer) diagrams
- Cross-functional maps; also known as swim lane diagrams
- Flowcharts

Each type of process map serves a purpose and one or all may be used in the course of a continual improvement journey. Regardless of form, the steps to produce a process map are the same. They are:

1. Define the boundaries of the process map
2. Create a simple list of activities starting each step with a verb
3. Sequence the activities
4. Draw the process map
5. Solicit feedback
6. Finalize the process map

7.1.1 High-level Integration Map

High-level integration maps show the relationships that exist between processes and can also be used to show the integration between associated tools.

A key benefit of a high-level integration map is that you can show the flow of information that occurs from one process to another.

High-level integration maps can be used in presentations and training materials to present a "high-level" view, before zooming in for more detail. Figure 7.1 shows a sample high-level integration map.

Quick Tip:	Keep it simple. Avoid including so many details that the map becomes unreadable.

7.1.2 Relationship Maps

Relationship maps show the supplier and customer relationships that exist within the boundaries of a process, the process activities, and the inputs and outputs produced.

Relationship maps may also be called SIPOC maps or diagrams. SIPOC diagrams are often used in the Six Sigma methodology.

A key benefit of a relationship map is that you can show, at a high level, how work flows across the major functions of an organization and the deliverables produced. Relationship maps can be used during process definition activities to gain consensus on the process stakeholders and deliverables. Figure 7.2 shows a sample relationship map.

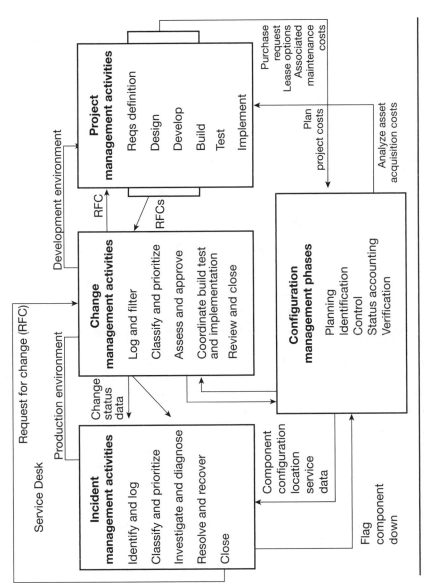

Figure 7.1   Sample high-level integration map

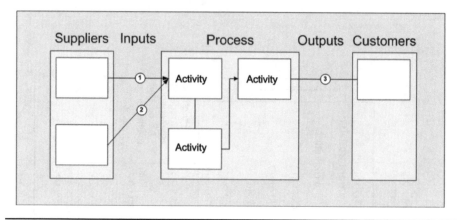

Figure 7.2 Sample relationship map

7.1.3 Cross-functional Map

Cross-functional maps, or swim lane diagrams, show the flow of process activities across the roles or major functions of an organization.

A key benefit of cross-functional maps is that you can show the inputs and outputs of each activity within a process, and the sequence of activities within a process, across the major functions of the business.

Cross-functional maps can be used during process design activities to illustrate in detail the flow of activities in a process from one function to the next. Figure 7.3 shows a sample cross-functional map. Cross-functional maps are an invaluable tool as they provide the visual clarity needed to eliminate bottlenecks, minimize handoffs, ensure activities are flowing in a logical sequence and so forth. To create a cross-functional process map:

- Assemble a team of stakeholders
- Use a large white board or place a large piece of paper on a wall
- Draw a horizontal band (swim lane) for each functional area or role involved in the process
  - Place the customer at the top
- Use Post-it notes to describe each step in the process
- Have each functional area place their Post-it notes on the draft process map
- Rearrange the Post-it notes until a consensus is reached indicating that:
  - All steps have been identified
  - The steps are arranged in the most logical sequence possible

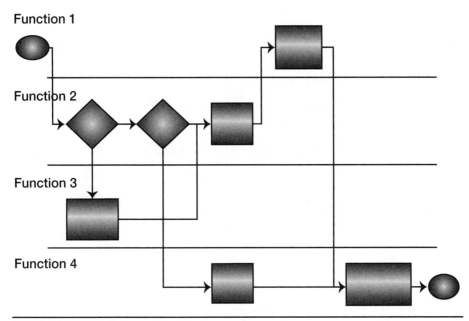

Figure 7.3 Sample cross-functional map

- Use flowcharting software to transcribe the map
- Add details such as labels, arrows, input descriptors, output descriptors, and decisions

7.1.4 Flowcharts

A flowchart is a diagram that shows the sequence of tasks that occur in a process. Flowcharts are one of the most common tools used to illustrate processes.

A key benefit of flowcharts is that you can show the sequence of activities within a process, decisions made within the boundaries of the process, and any decision loops that may occur. Flowcharts can be used during process design and improvement activities to illustrate the flow of activities in a process. Flowcharts can be as simple or as complex as needed to meet the needs of the target audience. Figure 7.4 shows a sample flowchart.

The American National Standards Institute (ANSI) has developed a standard set of symbols to be used when creating flowcharts. The most commonly used symbols are illustrated in Table 7.1. Using ANSI standard symbols ensures

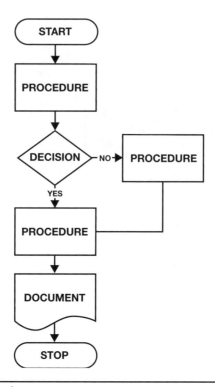

Figure 7.4   Sample flowchart

consistency and increases the readability of flowcharts, as does using the following techniques:

- Clearly designate the boundaries (start, stop) of the process
- Design the process to be read from left to right and from top to bottom
- At a minimum, make use of the most common applicable symbols
- Use verbs to describe the activities
- Keep the symbols a relatively equal distance apart to improve readability
- Label the outputs of your decision boxes (yes, no)
- Strive to direct the outputs of your decision boxes in a consistent manner (e.g., no = horizontal, yes = vertical)

Mistakes to avoid when producing flowcharts include:

- Producing "unbalanced" maps that have great detail in one area and very little detail in another
- Making them too complex rather than using off-page connectors
- Making them too small and not using white space to enhance readability
- Making them too busy

Table 7.1 Commonly-used ANSI symbols

(A)	On page connector
◯	Off page connector
▭	Single task or operation
◇	Decision—used in conjunction with result arrows
Yes ——— No ——▶	Yes and no result arrows
▯	Predefined process (represents another process that provides input or receives output from the current process)
▱	Information required to complete a task
▢	Process start and stop point

Common reasons for busy flowcharts include:

- Failing to identify sub-processes that can be used to break up the flowchart into logical sets of activities
- Incorporating existing processes into the flowchart rather than using the "predefined process" symbol
- Including checklists, procedures, or work instructions that may be more useful as documents or online help

Flowcharts are considered one of the seven basic tools of quality.

7.2 Seven Basic Tools of Quality

In 1950, American quality guru W. Edwards Deming went to Japan and trained hundreds of Japanese engineers, managers, and scholars in statistical process control. One of his students was a professor at the University of Tokyo named Kaoru Ishikawa.

Ishikawa had the desire to introduce the principles of quality control to all workers, and inspired by Deming's lectures, he developed what continue to be referred to today as the seven basic tools of quality. The **seven basic tools of quality** are simple but powerful data analysis tools that can be used to solve the majority of quality problems. Ishikawa believed that 90% of quality problems could be improved using these seven tools, and that most of these tools could be easily taught to any member of the organization. The seven basic tools of quality are:

- Cause-and-effect diagrams (also called Ishikawa or fishbone diagrams)
- Check sheets
- Control or run charts
- Flowcharts (discussed previously)
- Histograms
- Pareto charts
- Scatter diagrams

As is the case with process maps, each of these tools has a purpose and one or all may be used in the course of a continual improvement journey.

7.2.1 Cause-and-Effect Diagrams

A **cause-and-effect diagram**, also known as an Ishikawa diagram, is used to visually display the many potential causes for a specific problem or effect. Because of its shape, the cause-and-effect diagram may also be called a fishbone diagram. Figure 7.5 shows a sample cause-and-effect diagram.

A key benefit of a cause-and-effect diagram is that it facilitates a logical approach to problem solving by arranging potential causes into major categories. It helps you to think through and consider all of the possible causes of a problem, rather than just the most obvious ones. Categories may include:

- People, process, technology, information
- Process activities
- Who, what, when, where, why, and how

Cause-and-effect diagrams can be used during problem-solving activities to determine and categorize the cause of quality problems. To create a cause-and-effect diagram:

- Agree on the problem or effect to be analyzed

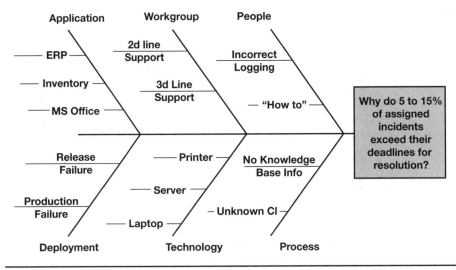

Figure 7.5   Sample cause-and-effect diagram

- Place the problem or effect to the right, or at the head of the diagram
- Identify all the broad categories of possible causes
- Extend vertical lines or "bones" from the spine of the diagram for each major category
- Brainstorm possible causes
- Use horizontal lines to record the possible causes for each category

At this point you can add metrics and data to the cause-and-effect diagram. For each major and possible cause, identify the number of times that the possible cause has occurred or been noticed. Record those numbers on the diagram next to each cause. You can then use the highest numbered items as starting points for further investigation. You can also transfer the information to a Pareto chart (discussed in Section 7.2.5).

7.2.2 Check Sheets

A **check sheet** is a structured, prepared form for collecting and analyzing data. Table 7.2 shows a sample check sheet.

A key benefit of a check sheet is that it can be adapted to a wide variety of purposes and used to quickly collect data required for analysis, typically for a short period of time. For example, an organization that does not have an incident management system may use a check sheet to determine the number of calls a service desk receives for a two week period. This information can then be used

Table 7.2 Sample check sheet

Service desk calls—Mary Brown						
Call type	**Day**					
	Mon	**Tues**	**Weds**	**Thurs**	**Fri**	**Total**
Hardware	√ √ √	√	√ √ √ √ √	√ √	√	12
Software	√ √ √ √ √	√ √ √ √	√ √	√ √ √ √	√ √ √ √	19
Network	√ √	√	√ √ √ √ √ √ √ √	√ √ √ √ √ √	√	18
Total	10	6	15	12	6	49

to develop a service desk staffing model. Capturing basic information about the types of calls received can also be used to develop a training plan.

Check sheets can be used to determine the frequency or patterns of events, problems, defects, etc. They are especially effective when used to quickly and easily gather data from a particular point in a process or in a repeatable situation experienced over time. To create a check sheet:

- Decide what event or problem will be observed
- Decide what data will be collected, when, and for how long
- Design a form that enables data to be recorded simply (e.g., by making check marks)
- Clearly label all of the spaces on the form
- Pilot the check sheet for a period of time to ensure it is easy to use and collects the required data
- Transfer the data to an automated system such as Microsoft Excel for further analysis

7.2.3 Control Charts

A **control chart** is a graph used to determine if a process is in a state of statistical control. Figure 7.6 shows a sample control chart.

Control charts contain reference lines that are determined by using historical data. These reference lines include:

- An upper control limit
- A center average
- A lower control limit

A control chart is a specific type of run chart. A **run chart** is a graph used to chart process variations over time. A key benefit of a control chart is that it can be used to distinguish significant process variations from normal process variations. For

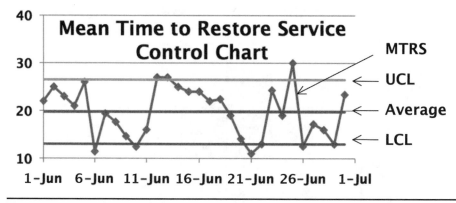

Figure 7.6 Sample control chart

example, a significant increase in the number of incidents reported to the service desk following a standard or minor change is not normal to the overall change management process. An increase within a predefined percentage, however, may be normal. Controls charts are used to study how a process changes over time and can be used to:

- Monitor process performance
- Determine whether process variations are consistent (in control) or inconsistent (out of control)
- Determine if variations can be avoided or require investigation
- Identify trends (positive or negative)
- Predict future process variations

To create a control chart:

- Identify a control point in the process where monitoring is needed
- Collect and chart data for your control point
- Use historical data to set the upper and lower control limits
- Create clear labels to enhance readability
- Automate the collection of data
- Chart data against the upper and lower control limits

7.2.4 Histograms

A **histogram** is a chart that shows the distribution of data into ranges or bins. For example, a histogram can be used to show the distribution of scores that learners receive on an exam in increments of 10, as illustrated in Figure 7.7. A histogram is a form of bar chart that uses quantitative (versus categorical) data.

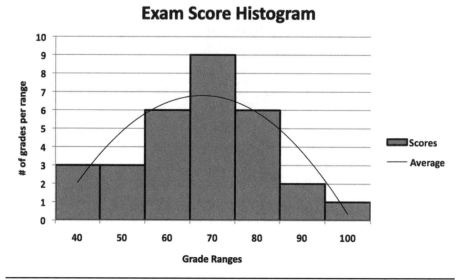

Figure 7.7 Sample histogram

---

*A **bar chart** is a chart used to compare two or more values that fall into discrete categories. Data for a bar chart is categorical (versus quantitative) data that cannot be placed into numerical bins.*

A key benefit of a histogram is that it provides an easy way to see the distribution of data in relation to a target value. Histograms are used to study the distribution of data in relation to predefined targets. Just as exams have a target pass rate; processes have a target value that indicates where the output of the process should fall. The center of the distribution in a histogram should fall on or near this target value. If it does not, process improvement may be required.

Histograms can also be used to assess the effects of process changes. For example, a histogram can be used during the pilot phase of a project to chart the ability of a redesigned process to fall within the target range. To create a histogram:

- Determine the data to be charted
- Determine how many bins there should be for the given amount of data
- Ensure each bin represents an equal increment of distribution
- Create clear labels to enhance readability

| **Quick Tip:** | Take care when determining the bins to be used in a histogram as too few or too many bars can skew the results. |

7.2.5 Pareto Charts

A **Pareto chart** is a chart that shows the cumulative frequency of values plotted in a descending order. A Pareto chart is a form of bar chart that puts data in a hierarchical order. Figure 7.8 shows a sample Pareto chart.

A key benefit of a Pareto chart is that it provides an easy way to see the distribution of problem causes. Pareto charts are used to highlight the most important among a set of problem causes, such as the most common source of errors affecting an application, or the most common customer complaints.

Based on a principle first developed by Vilfredo Pareto, a turn-of-the-century Italian economist who examined a society's wealth, the **Pareto principle**, also known as the **80-20 Rule**, when related to quality improvement states that 80% of problems usually stem from 20% of the causes. A Pareto chart enables the most frequently occurring causes to be identified and then prioritized for improvement. By concentrating on the 20% of the causes, you can focus time, effort, and resources to achieve the greatest results.

To create a Pareto chart:

- Determine the data to be charted
- When applicable, determine the categories to be used to group data
- Select a measurement such as cost, quality, frequency, or time
- Determine what period of time the Pareto chart will cover such as one day, one week, or one month

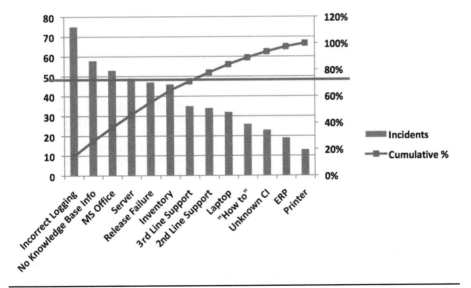

Figure 7.8 Sample Pareto chart

- Collect and chart the data in descending order of occurrence
- Create clear labels to enhance readability

Quick Tip:	Pareto charts work especially well when coupled with the results of a cause-and-effect diagram.

7.2.6 Scatter Diagrams

A **scatter diagram**, also known as a scatter plot, is a graph used to show how two pairs of variables are related. If the variables reflected in the scatter diagram are strongly related, or correlated, the points will fall along a line or curve. The stronger the correlation, the tighter the points will hug the line. Figure 7.9 shows a sample scatter diagram. A key benefit of a scatter diagram is that it provides an easy way to test for cause-and-effect relationships.

While scatter diagrams cannot be used to prove that one variable causes a change in the other, they can be used to study the relationship between the two. For example, a scatter diagram can be used to determine if reducing the amount of testing that is done when making changes results in an increase in the number of incidents caused by those changes.

Data used for a scatter diagram must be of similar types—quantitative or categorical—or the results will be skewed and produce a false relationship.

To create a scatter diagram:

- Collect data samples for two suspected pairs of related data
- Plot the first variable (the cause variable) on the horizontal axis with its values increasing from left to right
- Plot the second variable (the effect variable) on the vertical axis and increase its values as you move from bottom to top
- Create clear labels to enhance readability

Quick Tip:	A key to success is to validate the needs of the target audience prior to designing and developing reports. Agree upon and document the details of each report including its purpose, audience, and data elements, along with associated calculations and run times. Chapter 8 discusses producing meaningful metrics and reports in greater detail.

Quick Tip:	Tools such as Microsoft Excel or statistical analysis software can be used to automatically produce charts such as control charts, histograms, Pareto charts, and scatter diagrams. Schedule the report to run at the agreed upon times and transition it to the production environment under the control of change management.

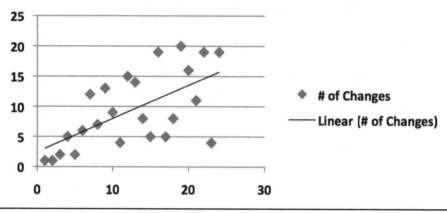

Figure 7.9   Sample scatter diagram

7.3 Miscellaneous Tools and Techniques

A number of additional tools and techniques may be used in the course of a process design or improvement project. These include:

- Business cases
- Return on investment calculations
- RACI matrices

These tools and techniques are sometimes viewed as unnecessary, particularly in smaller projects; however, such a view may be short sighted. Informal projects are often viewed as unimportant and so each of these tools and techniques, even if executed in a simple way, ensure process design and improvement activities occur in a controlled and appropriately formal manner.

7.3.1 Producing a Business Case

Step 2 of the ten process design and improvement steps involves establishing a project and forming a project team. For larger projects, a business case that describes the reasons the change is being considered may be required to establish a project. New processes and significant changes to existing processes may prompt the need to produce a business case to justify and articulate the reason for the change. In other words, a business case answers questions such as:

- Why is the project needed?
- What is the recommended solution?

- What assumptions or constraints are reflected in the recommended solution?
- How will the recommended solution address the challenges and opportunities facing the organization?
- What are the benefits?
- What are the risks?
- When and how will the solution be deployed?
- How much time, effort, and money will be needed to deliver the solution and realize the benefits?
- What is the cost of doing nothing?

Benefits of producing a business case include:

- The project team has a vehicle for capturing what has been learned about the current environment, along with assumptions and conclusions regarding how the project will benefit the business
- Management is provided the information needed to approve and fund the project including the costs, benefits, and risks
- All stakeholders are provided a high-level description of the project and its likely consequences

The likely consequences of a project may be benefits or they may be risks that must be considered and managed. A **risk** is a possible event that could cause injury or loss or affect the ability to realize a benefit.

> *ITIL describes risk as uncertainty of outcome, whether positive opportunity or negative threat. This definition is interesting because it not only requires determining how to mitigate negative risks, it also begs the question, "What if we are wildly successful?"*

Project benefits may include tangible and intangible benefits. A **tangible benefit** is capable of being measured precisely. Tangible benefits are typically expressed in financial terms. An **intangible benefit** is a benefit that cannot be measured precisely. Tangible benefits that may be described in a business case include:

- Increased availability of IT services
- Increased productivity
- Reduced risk
- Increased efficiency
- Increased effectiveness
- Improved resource utilization
- Increased reliability
- Reduced cycle time

Intangible benefits that may be described in a business case include:

- Increased customer satisfaction
- Improved customer relations
- Enhanced customer self-sufficiency
- Increased employee satisfaction
- Improved morale
- Improved decision making
- Increased knowledge
- Improved collaboration and communication
- More accurate solutions
- More proactive services

Both tangible and intangible benefits are important and a business case should reflect them in a balanced, customer-focused way. Project risks reflected in a business case may include:

- Insufficient resources (project, ongoing)
- Lack of management commitment
- Insufficient budget
- Insufficient commitment to training
- Corporate politics
- Disruption to the production environment

An effective business case tells a story and provides the reader with a clear vision or picture of the proposed future state. Table 7.3 shows the structure of a business case.

7.3.2 Calculating Return on Investment

Return on investment (ROI) measures the benefit derived from an investment—such as a process improvement project—and compares it with the total cost of the project.

ROI = Net Benefits / Project Investment

ROI is typically expressed as a percentage, calculated as follows:

ROI% = (Net Benefits / Project Investment) x 100

In its simplest form, calculating ROI considers only financial costs and benefits. Calculating ROI can be much more complex, however, and should consider intangible as well as tangible benefits. Complex ROI calculations can be time

Table 7.3 Sample business case structure

Sample business case structure
Introduction—introduces the project—its scope and background
Opportunities and assumptions—describes the business drivers prompting the proposed solution along with underlying assumptions
Recommended solution—describes the recommended approach and, where applicable, proposed alternate approaches
Risks and contingencies—describes project risks, probabilities, and mitigation tactics
Required resources—describes the resources needed to execute the project and realize the proposed benefits
Commitments—describes the project milestones, reporting mechanisms, deliverables schedule, and budget schedule
Value proposition—describes and quantifies the business benefits, costs, and projected return on investment

consuming and so are typically reserved for larger projects. Even in its simplest form, ROI is a useful way to communicate the value of an investment and answer the questions:

- What do I get in return for my investment?
- Is the return worth the investment?

Quick Tip:	ROI can be calculated prior to the start of a project and used to justify the investment. It should also be calculated post-project and used to communicate the benefits realized. When ROI was not calculated pre-project, it can still be used post-project to show proof of concept and gain support for future initiatives.

Calculating ROI is not the same as a cost benefit analysis. A **cost benefit analysis** compares the costs and benefits of two or more potential solutions. Like ROI, in its simplest form, cost benefit analysis considers only financial costs and financial benefits. Financial costs may be nonrecurring (one time) or recurring (ongoing). A more complex cost benefit analysis considers intangible benefits as well.

The goal of a cost benefit analysis is to answer the questions:

- Which of the proposed solutions meets the needs of the business?
- Is the proposed solution worth the cost?

7.3.3 Creating a RACI Matrix

A RACI matrix maps the roles and responsibilities of the various people and teams engaged in performing a process, with the activities of the process. A RACI matrix can also be used to map roles and responsibilities to project activities or tasks. Table 7.4 shows a sample RACI matrix.

With regard to process activities, a RACI matrix illustrates what role is:

- **Responsible** for executing the activity
- **Accountable** for the outcome of the activity (i.e., the owner)
- **Consulted** during the process to obtain information or knowledge
- **Informed** or kept up-to-date about process activities

Expanded forms of RACI include:

- **RACIVS** which reflects who verifies that an outcome meets acceptance criteria and who signs off on the verified outcome
- **RASCI** which reflects a support role allocated to a responsible role

A RACI matrix is an invaluable tool as it:

- Helps clarify activities and tasks in a process
- Helps ensure all stakeholders are identified and engaged
- Reduces bad decisions by ensuring the correct people are involved
- Determines accountability for activities
- Encourages teamwork by clarifying roles and responsibilities
- Reduces misunderstandings
- Identifies and enables the elimination of duplicated effort
- Clarifies handoffs and process boundaries
- Enables people to understand the role they play in a process
- Provides a cross-functional view for everyone involved in a process
- Improves acceptance of the new process

Table 7.4 Sample RACI matrix

Incident management tasks	SD	Tech mgmt	User	App mgmt
Incident recording	A, R C I	I	C,I	I
Incident matching	A,R,C,I		C,I	
Incident categorization and prioritization	A,R,C,I	C,I	C,I	C,I
Initial diagnosis	A,R, C,I	C,I	C,I	C,I
Assignment to 2nd/3rd level	A,R,C,I	C	C,I	C
Investigation and diagnosis	A,R, C,I	R,C,I	C,I	R,C,I
Close incident	A,R,C,I	R C, I	C,I	R C, I

To create a RACI matrix:

- List all of the roles involved in a process (matrix columns)
- List all process activities (matrix rows)
- Fill in the matrix using the codes R, A, C, and I to define the relationship between the roles and the activities
- Analyze the matrix

Things to consider when analyzing a RACI matrix include:

- Every row must contain only one A
- Every row must contain one A and one R
- A role can be both accountable and responsible for an activity
- Too many A's assigned to a single role may overwhelm that role or may result in a bottleneck
- No R's in a row indicates a gap in the process
- No R's in a row may mean the task is not needed
- A role with no R's or A's may mean the role is not needed
- Consulting too many people may cause inefficiency and prove to be disruptive:
  - Can procedures be provided?
  - Can a knowledgebase be provided?
- Having to inform too many people may cause excessive work:
  - Can people be informed only when exceptions occur?
  - Can people be informed automatically?

Quick Tip:	To improve readability, list the roles with the A's and the most R's towards the left side of the matrix.

Creating a RACI matrix not only provides a way to assign roles and responsibilities to process activities, it also helps ensure that:

- Only the people or teams that should be engaged are engaged
- Individuals or teams are not overburdened by taking on too many roles or responsibilities

A RACI matrix should be considered a "living" document that is refined as process design and improvement activities proceed. It can be used during the project to:

- Determine needed changes to departmental goals and individual job descriptions
- Design workflow automation
- Design automated tasks to inform roles as needed
- Create an organizational level agreement (OLA)

An output of the service level management process, OLAs can be used to clarify responsibilities when a row on a RACI matrix has multiple R's.

If the benefits are so great, why isn't this technique used more often? Producing a RACI matrix is time-consuming and can be quite difficult as people or teams accept or reject responsibility for their role. However, there is an old expression, "pay me now, or pay me later." Such is the case with a RACI matrix. These roles and responsibilities must be clarified. Accountability must be defined. Optimally, that is done prior to implementing a process. If not, battles ensue, work is delayed, and reaching a consensus invariably takes much longer. The next chapter discusses additional techniques that can be used to manage the discomfort that often accompanies organizational change.

Summary

A variety of proven tools and techniques can be used to document, design, and continually improve processes. The effective use of these tools and techniques requires: people skilled in their use, involvement by the people who perform the processes, and the commitment of management to continual improvement.

Process mapping is a highly effective technique for making work visible. Process maps show the sequence of tasks that occur within a process, and also the relationship one process has with other processes. They provide a visual representation for people working within processes, or for people working on processes in the course of process design and improvement.

Process maps can assume several forms including: high-level integration maps, relationship maps, cross-functional maps, and flowcharts. Each type of process map serves a purpose and one or all may be used in the course of a continual improvement journey.

The seven basic tools of quality are simple but powerful data analysis tools that can be used to solve the majority of quality problems. The seven tools are: cause-and-effect diagrams, check sheets, control charts, flowcharts, histograms, Pareto charts, and scatter diagrams. As is the case with process maps, each tool serves a purpose and one or all may be used for continual improvement.

For larger process design or improvement projects, a business case may be used to describe the reasons for the proposed change, along with associated benefits (both tangible and intangible), costs, and risks. A business case typically includes the expected ROI.

ROI measures the benefit derived from an investment and compares it with the total cost of the project. ROI can be calculated prior to the start of a project and used to justify the investment, and then post-project for use communicating the benefits realized. When ROI was not calculated pre-project, it can still be used post-project to show proof of concept and gain support for future initiatives.

A RACI matrix maps the roles and responsibilities of the various people and teams engaged in performing a process, with the activities of the process. Relative to process activities, a RACI matrix illustrates who is responsible, accountable, consulted, or informed. A RACI matrix has many benefits and can be used in a variety of ways during a project. It should be considered a "living" document that is refined as process design and improvement activities proceed.

Discussion Topics

- Process mapping and the seven basic tools of quality are proven tools and techniques. Why aren't they used more often?
- Calculating ROI is an effective way to gain support for a project. What tangible and intangible benefits can be used to calculate the ROI of ITSM?
- A RACI matrix helps clarify roles and responsibilities. What are the consequences of failing to clarify roles and responsibilities?

Review Questions

1. What is the difference between a high-level integration map and a relationship map?
2. Briefly describe the purpose of a cross-functional map.
3. Describe three ways to avoid busy flowcharts.
4. What is a key benefit of a cause-and-effect diagram?
5. List the three types of reference lines needed to create a control chart.
6. When using a histogram, what outcome may indicate that process improvement is necessary?
7. Explain the Pareto principle relative to quality improvement.
8. What are the benefits of producing a business case?
9. What is the difference between ROI and cost benefit analysis?
10. List four ways a RACI matrix can be used during a project.

WAV Web Added Value™

This book has free material available for download from the Web Added Value™ resource center at *www.jrosspub.com*

8

Producing Meaningful Metrics

The purpose of every process is to produce an outcome that is of value to its customer. Metrics provide the ability to determine how capable a process is of producing the desired outcome (i.e., how capable it is of creating value).

A metric is a performance measure.

Metrics can be used to control, measure, predict, and improve process performance. They can be used to assess all aspects of a process including inputs, outputs, and activities. Like calculating the return on an investment, they can be used to measure both tangible and intangible process characteristics. Metrics can also be used to measure attainment of strategic (long term), tactical (shorter term), and operational (day-to-day) performance goals. Meaningful metrics help measure process characteristics such as:

- **Compliance:** Are we following the process?
- **Quality:** Are we executing the process effectively?
- **Performance:** Are we executing the process efficiently?
- **Value:** Is what we are doing facilitating business goals and objectives?

As illustrated in Figure 8.1, the most common types of process metrics include:

- **Efficiency:** A measure used to compare the value of a process (its effectiveness) with its cost
- **Effectiveness:** A measure used to show the capability of a process to deliver value (i.e., produce a desired output)

117

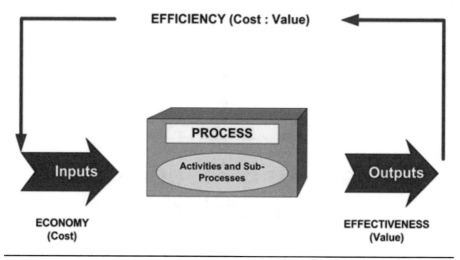

Figure 8.1   Common process metric types

- **Cost:** Also known as economy, a measure used to show the cost of the process inputs required to produce the desired outputs

Efficiency, effectiveness, and cost are each important and a common mistake is to view them as mutually exclusive. Increasing efficiency, for example, is about saving time and reducing costs. But to what end? Effectiveness is about delivering quality and satisfying customer requirements. But does that mean no matter how long it takes or how much it costs? A process that becomes too efficient may become ineffective and vice versa and so measuring each metric type is important.

The demands of today's work world make it more important than ever to measure and continually improve process performance. These demands include the need to:

- Satisfy customers' ever-rising expectations
- Demonstrate compliance with regulatory controls
- Cut or maintain costs
- Optimize staffing levels
- Increase overall performance
- Do more with less

Well-designed and meaningful metrics can be used to:

- Justify existing or additional resources
- Compare performance against:
  - A baseline
  - A target or goal
  - Another organization

- Demonstrate proof of concept
- Initiate corrective action when needed

What are well-designed and meaningful metrics? The Process Maturity Framework (PMF) can be used to answer that question. This is because the ability to measure the performance of a process is one of the characteristics the PMF uses to assess the maturity of processes.

Table 8.1 illustrates that when a process is in the *initial* level of maturity, it is common that few results are being retained. As a process moves through the *repeatable, defined,* and *managed* maturity levels, organizations recognize the need to set objectives and measure achievements against targets. At the *optimizing* level, processes are being continually improved to ensure alignment with business goals.

So what is a well-designed and meaningful metric? It is a metric that reflects a strategic objective and is aligned with business goals.

8.1 Producing Meaningful Metrics: Common Practice

Designing and producing meaningful metrics is easier said than done. Common practice is that organizations:

- Measure what they can given available data
- Focus on operational performance
- Manually produce reports

Measuring what they can—versus what they should to demonstrate alignment with business goals—is a typical characteristic of an organization that lacks a process orientation. The most classic example is service availability. Since the earliest days of computing, IT organizations have reported on availability. What's historically been lacking, however, is a true end-to-end service perspective. IT may report on server availability, for example, but not reflect in that metric network availability or the availability of other components used to deliver the service end-to-end. While reporting component availability is important from an IT perspective, it often leaves the business asking, "Who cares?"

Table 8.1 Metrics and the ITIL Process Maturity Framework

Optimizing	• Strategic objectives are aligned with business goals
Managed	• Objectives and targets are based on business goals
Defined	• Agreed-upon objectives and targets
Repeatable	• No clear objectives or formal targets
Initial	• Few results retained

So too does focusing on operational, or day-to-day performance metrics. Again, while tracking a technician's performance during incident resolution is important, the business is much more interested in the IT organization's ability to prioritize activities and deliver services that meet agreed targets.

It is common for organizations to manually produce metrics, particularly when processes are first being defined and designed. The act of manually producing metrics and performance reports has many downsides including that it is:

- Labor intensive
- Error prone
- Slow

Every day IT and business executives make decisions that require timely and accurate information. In the absence of well-designed and meaningful metrics, executives are forced to use recommendations and staff input that may—or may not—be accurate and unbiased to make decisions.

8.2 Producing Meaningful Metrics: Best Practice

Done right, metrics and performance reports enable:

- Fact-based decision making
- Governance
- Early detection of performance problems
- Continual improvement

Each of the ITSM and quality management frameworks, standards, and models previously discussed recognize the need to monitor, measure, and review performance metrics. One of the most widely recognized quality assurance and improvement models is the Deming Cycle, which involves executing four steps: plan, do, check, and act. The Deming Cycle is imbedded in ISO/IEC 20000 and the *check* step requires that organizations have in place:

- Methods for monitoring and measuring ITSM processes
- The ability to show that processes achieve planned results
- Planned reviews and audits to ensure that processes:
  - Conform to the ITSM plan
  - Are effectively implemented and maintained

Best practices for satisfying these requirements include:

- Implementing a metrics program
- Using metrics to achieve business and process improvement goals
- Automatically monitoring metrics and publishing reports

8.2.1 Implementing a Metrics Program

It's quite common for management and staff to latch onto a single metric and deem that metric the most important. The upside of such an approach is that the organization is focused on a specific improvement opportunity. The downside of such a singular focus is that it can drive negative behavior. An emphasis on efficiency, for example, very often results in reduced effectiveness.

A **metrics program** or measurement framework describes the metrics needed to achieve business goals, how to collect them, and how to use them to continually improve performance. Examples of metrics programs include the Balanced Scorecard and Results that Matter approaches.

The Balanced Scorecard: A well-known and commonly used metrics program is the Balanced Scorecard. Popularized by Drs. Robert Kaplan and David Norton of the Harvard Business School in the 1990s, the **Balanced Scorecard** is a performance measurement framework that combines strategic non-financial performance measures with traditional financial metrics. The Balanced Scorecard approach suggests that organizations develop and analyze metrics relative to four key perspectives: financial, customer, internal business processes, learning and growth. This approach gives executives and managers a more balanced view of organizational performance.

Results that Matter: Popularized by the book *Results that Matter: Improving Communities by Engaging Citizens, Measuring Performance, and Getting Things Done* (Jossey-Bass, 2005), many government agencies are implementing performance measurement initiatives aimed at ensuring every department within the government has the tools and data needed for all employees to focus on delivering **results that matter** to citizens.

A metrics program uses a top-down approach to ensure that performance metrics support business objectives and performance improvement goals. An effective metrics program encompasses:

- What you *should* measure to achieve business goals
- Individual process performance
- Process interfaces

Ten steps for creating a metrics program include:

- **Step 1:** Determine management's vision—identify strategic and measurable goals and objectives
- **Step 2:** Identify critical success factors—decompose the strategic goals and objectives into measurable results that must happen for processes to support the stated goals and objectives
- **Step 3:** Identify key performance indicators—identify the key measures to be used to monitor and measure process performance
- **Step 4:** Identify metrics—identify the measures to be used to monitor and measure process performance

- **Step 5:** Verify that metrics are *SMART*—ensure metrics are specific, measurable, achievable, relevant, and timely
- **Step 6:** Identify required data elements—identify the data elements required to produce the metrics and assess their accuracy
- **Step 7:** Test and pilot your metrics and reports—verify that metrics and reports are statistically valid and satisfy customer requirements
- **Step 8:** Document your metrics and reports—include its identity (e.g., unique name), purpose, audience, and associated data elements
- **Step 9:** Place approved metrics and reports under change management control—ensure proposed changes are assessed for impact
- **Step 10:** Continually review reports for effectiveness—continually ensure metrics and reports are aligned with business goals

This approach is used to determine the critical success factors (CSFs), key performance indicators (KPIs), and metrics for each process relative to each business goal. (Appendix D provides sample KPIs for each ISO/IEC 20000 process.)

Quick Tip:	Use common reporting tools such as pie and bar charts to regularly assess data accuracy. Are data elements being specified accurately? Is "other" being used appropriately? Are individuals within a team or function specifying data elements consistently? Ensure that training covers not only how to log data, but how to log that data accurately and consistently as well.

Roles that will be involved in defining CSFs, KPIs, and metrics include:

- **Service management program owner**—responsible for overall program
- **Process owners**—responsible for process specific metrics
- **Process stakeholders**—responsible for validating metrics and participating in baselining activities
- **Data analysts**—responsible for ensuring the needed data is captured, summarized, and assembled into appropriate reports and graphs
- **Technical specialists**—responsible for facilitating the implementation and administration of associated technologies

8.2.2 Using Metrics to Achieve Business and Process Improvement Goals

Can you have too many metrics? Absolutely! Some organizations measure every aspect of a process, but fail to ensure the process is contributing to the greater business goals. The end result is that people may be working very hard, but not really working on the right things.

Any number of metrics may be used to measure process characteristics such as cost, quality, efficiency, and effectiveness. However, it is recommended that no more than two to three CSFs and KPIs are defined at any given point in time. Limiting the number of KPIs makes it possible to (1) focus peoples' efforts on what is important and (2) measure the effect of process changes aimed at improving a particular process characteristic. In an effort to drive positive behavior, it is common for organizations to tie performance plans and incentives to CSFs and KPIs. Figure 8.2 illustrates deconstructing a CSF for the change management process into KPIs and metrics.

Among all the performance measures available to managers to change peoples' behavior and move the organization in a new direction, CSFs and KPIs are the most powerful. Care must be taken when selecting CSFs and KPIs to ensure peoples' efforts are focused on doing the right things right.

Be careful what you ask for!	

Quick Tip:	An important step is to reflect metrics in employee job descriptions and performance plans and, when possible, provide appropriate incentives. Failing to take such a step invariably results in a disconnect between desired and actual behavior.

Vision
- Strategy, goals, and objectives
- Deliver cost-effective services in a competitive timeframe

CSF
- What must happen to achieve process success
- Make changes quickly and accurately

KPI
- Key metric used to manage a process
- Reduce the number of emergency changes
- Increase the number of standard changes

Metric
- What is measured to manage a process
- Number of changes by type

Figure 8.2   Sample CSFs, KPIs, and metrics for change management

Measuring Individual Performance

How management uses metrics influences their effectiveness. Having too many metrics that lack meaning typically means the staff is being required to capture more data than is needed. Using metrics to point fingers or punish will decrease moral and drive bad behavior. Common complaints and concerns from IT staff include:

- I'm entering all this data and no one is using it
- The data I'm entering is being used as a stick to criticize and find fault with my work
- The data being collected is not useful to me
- Process efficiency is just another word for downsizing

All of these complaints, when true, are valid and must be addressed. To avoid these complaints, management must use the data being collected to improve first and foremost, the quality of service being delivered to the business, but also the feeling of job satisfaction experienced by the IT staff. Management must communicate honestly with staff about its efforts to optimize staffing levels and ensure the IT organization has the skills needed to achieve ITSM goals.

It is also important to use performance metrics to drive continual improvement, rather than doing whatever it takes to "make the numbers right," or keep management and customers happy. A spirit of learning, growth, and continual improvement will drive behavior that is consistent with corporate objectives, rather than conflicting behaviors that could arise if one person's measures are at odds with another's.

Measuring Process Integration

Every ITSM process has a relationship with:

- Every other ITSM process
- Other IT processes such as project management
- Other business processes such as financial management

To achieve higher levels of process maturity, these interfaces must be recognized and continually monitored, measured, and improved.

It is also important to recognize the impact that integrated processes can have on a single process. Figure 8.3 illustrates the positive effect that integrated processes can have on the number of incidents affecting the production environment.

Conversely, immature processes, or the absence of processes, can cause the opposite effect. An ineffective change management process, for example, is often the most common cause of incidents.

Successes as a result of process integration must be clearly communicated to: (1) recognize accomplishments, (2) show proof of concept, and (3) provide incentive to continually improve. For example:

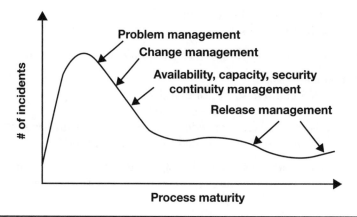

Figure 8.3 The positive effect of process integration on metrics

By integrating incident management with problem and change management:

- Number of incidents being reported has decreased by X%
- Time to resolve incidents has decreased by X%
- First line resolution has increased by X%
- Customer satisfaction has increased by X%

By integrating incident management with service level management:

- Number of priority 1 incidents being reported has decreased by X%
- Nnumber of customers contacting IT staff outside the service desk has decreased by X% (may be difficult to fully capture but is worth attempting)

Since the output of one process is the input to another, process design and improvement efforts must consider the effect of changes on all integrated processes.

Quick Tip:	Use the seven basic tools of quality to analyze performance and seek out trends. Each of these tools has a purpose and, used properly, serves as the foundation of an effective metrics program.

8.2.3 Automatically Monitoring Metrics and Publishing Reports

A sign of maturity is being able to automatically monitor metrics and publish reports. Automated reporting:

- Reduces the effort required to manually produce reports

- Reduces the number of errors reflected in reports
- Increases the timeliness of reports

The ability to automate reporting begins with understanding:

- What data is available?
- What is the definitive source of that data?
- Is the data located in disparate systems?
- What tools are available or needed to aggregate and summarize the data?
- What tools are available or needed to produce reports?

This simple set of questions provides insight into the fact that automatically monitoring metrics and publishing reports is easier said than done. To automate metrics and reports:

1. Identify the data sources
2. Identify and document the algorithms
3. Design reports that meet audience needs and aid understanding
4. Place the reports under change management control
5. Determine the appropriate distribution medium
6. Schedule and automate report distribution

Review metrics regularly to ensure they are worth the time spent collecting data, producing reports, and analyzing and acting upon the results. Involve all stakeholders to determine what is needed (i.e., what is meaningful) and what is sustainable.

8.3 The Role of Service Level Management

Service level management is a critical process as it determines targets for all ITSM processes. Unlike CSFs and KPIs that reflect goals and a future state, targets reflect the operational performance metrics that are agreed upon in SLAs.

Each process owner works with service level management to understand the **service level requirements (SLRS)**, or customer requirements, and considers those requirements during process design and improvement activities. Figure 8.4 illustrates how options for satisfying the requirements must be considered during process design or redesign, along with the cost of satisfying those requirements.

A fundamental premise of ITSM is that the business must be willing to fund the resources needed to satisfy requirements. For example, if the business requires that all incidents reported by a particular business area be viewed as priority 1 incidents, the business must be willing to fund the resources needed to satisfy that requirement.

Once targets are understood, milestones can be identified that can be used to monitor process performance, reflect control points along the way, and proactively ensure the targets can be met. These milestones may be recorded in OLAs

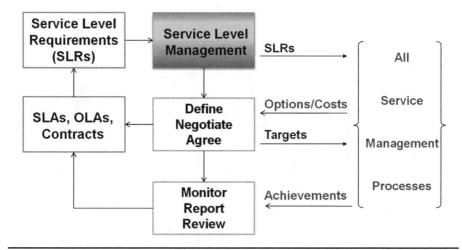

Figure 8.4   Using SLRs during process design and improvement activities

for internal organizations, or in contracts for external organizations. Figure 8.5 illustrates using metrics to monitor and ensure SLA compliance.

OLAs and contracts ensure each of the stakeholder groups involved in a process understands its role, responsibilities, and associated targets. Table 8.2 shows sample OLA metrics.

Metrics tied to OLAs and contracts can be used to ensure targets are being met or to trigger an improvement plan. Having stakeholders work together to determine the appropriate metrics to monitor is an effective way to initiate more positive communication between groups and manage expectations relative to results.

8.4 Keys to a Successful Metrics Program

Producing metrics based on what you can (vs. should) measure, or on what you think management and customers want to see (but aren't sure) is a waste of time and will do little to help the organization mature and improve. Well-designed and meaningful metrics drive positive behaviors and can be used to demonstrate an ROI on process design and improvement activities.

Keys to success include:

- Ensure metrics are meaningful and aligned with business goals
- Use baseline metrics and indicators or thresholds initially rather than nothing at all
- Keep it simple—produce metrics that are "good enough" to control, monitor, and predict performance

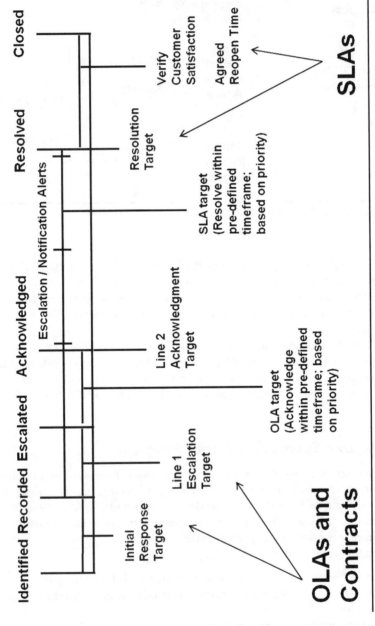

Figure 8.5   Using metrics to monitor and ensure SLA compliance

Table 8.2 Sample OLA metrics

Service desk	Sample target
Response within target	99%
Resolved on initial contact	85%
Reopened	<5%
Assigned within target	98%
Assigned correctly	Increasing
Overall quality	>4 (out of 5)
Desktop support	**Sample target**
Status requests—unrecorded incidents	Reducing
Acknowledged within target	98%
Status alerts per incident	<2
Reassigned after 75% of target	<2%
Resolved within SLA target	99%
Reopened	<5%
Overall quality	>4 (out of 5)

- Automate metrics collection as much as possible
- Analyze performance and seek out trends
- Use metrics to provide constructive, timely feedback

The most effective metrics programs foster an honest appraisal of the current environment, trigger constructive feedback and communication, and enable the continual alignment of process and business goals. If metrics are moving in the wrong direction, investigate quickly and determine an appropriate course of action. If metrics are moving in a positive direction—even if only slightly—celebrate that fact and encourage continued progress.

Use a variety of methods to communicate performance and initiate a two-way dialog about how performance can be improved. Methods may include:

- Themes
- Presentations
- Dashboards
- Reports
- Portals/intranets
- Newsletters

An effective metrics program provides all stakeholders the ability to assess performance and see and understand the results of their efforts. Metrics can be a starting point for problem-solving, relationship building, and communication. The act of sitting down to discuss what metrics are needed and determining CSFs and KPIs alone is a positive step in the right direction.

The organizational change management activities discussed in the next section help to keep everyone moving in the same direction.

Summary

The purpose of every process is to produce an outcome that is of value to its customer. Metrics can be used to control, measure, predict, and improve process performance. Meaningful metrics help measure process characteristics such as: compliance, quality, performance, and value. The most common types of metrics are: efficiency, effectiveness, and cost. Each of these metric types can influence the others thus measuring them all is important.

Well-designed and meaningful metrics are tied to strategic objectives and continually improved. Best practices for designing and improving meaningful metrics include: implementing a metrics program, using metrics to achieve business and process improvement goals, and automatically monitoring metrics and producing reports.

Creating a metrics program involves a ten step, top-down approach aimed at ensuring performance metrics support business objectives and performance improvement goals. Key steps include determining management's vision, determining CSFs, and then deconstructing CSFs into KPIs and metrics. Approved metrics and associated reports should be placed under change management control and reviewed regularly for effectiveness.

A sign of maturity is being able to automatically monitor metrics and publish reports. Automated reporting reduces the effort required to produce reports, reduces the number of errors reflected in reports, and increases the timeliness of reports. Automated reporting requires a comprehensive understanding of the data and tools available or needed to produce reports.

Service level management is a critical process as it defines targets for all ITSM processes. Unlike CSFs and KPIs that reflect goals and a future state, targets reflect the operational performance metrics that are agreed upon in service level agreements. OLAs and contracts ensure each of the stakeholder groups involved in a process understands its role and responsibilities and associated targets.

Well-designed and meaningful metrics drive positive behaviors and can be used to demonstrate an ROI on process design and improvement activities. A variety of methods should be used to communicate performance and initiate a two-way dialog about how performance can be improved. Organizational change management activities can be used to keep everyone moving in the same direction.

Discussion Topics

- Metrics such as efficiency, effectiveness, and cost can influence each other. What are the consequences of placing too great an emphasis on cost?
- Care must be taken to ensure metrics are worth the time and effort. What factors influence an organization's ability to produce meaningful metrics?
- How management uses metrics influences their effectiveness. How can metrics be used to increase the morale of an organization?

Review Questions

1. Meaningful metrics help measure what four process characteristics?
2. List and describe the three most common metric types.
3. How do organizations view metrics at the *defined* level of maturity?
4. What is the downside of focusing on a single metric?
5. Define the term *metrics program* and provide two examples.
6. What is the first step to take when creating a metrics program?
7. True or false. You can have too many metrics. Explain your answer.
8. How can management address valid complaints from IT staff regarding how metrics are used?
9. Why is measuring process integration important?
10. Describe the role service level management plays in producing metrics.

This book has free material available for download from the
Web Added Value™ resource center at *www.jrosspub.com*

9

Managing Organizational Change

Change is inevitable and, to some degree, so is the discomfort associated with change. This is particularly true when the change is major, such as when a new process is implemented or when an existing process is significantly modified. Change is also essential to an organization's ability to mature and grow therefore efforts must be taken to support and encourage workers throughout the change in an effort to:

- Maximize the benefits of the change
- Minimize the risks

The term change management is often used in today's work world and its meaning can vary. For example, in the context of ITSM, change management is the process responsible for ensuring changes to IT services are assessed, approved, implemented, and reviewed in a controlled manner.

In the context of process design, implementation, and improvement, change management is often referred to as organizational change management (OCM). OCM is the process of preparing, motivating, and equipping people to meet new business challenges.

Major changes such as new or significantly changed processes will require stakeholders throughout the organization to assume new responsibilities, learn new skills, and adopt new behaviors. It will take time for people to accept these new roles thus OCM activities must:

- Promote awareness and understanding of why the change is needed
- Encourage a willingness to support and participate in the change
- Help people understand the benefits of the change

133

- Help people understand how to change
- Provide the education and training people need to learn new skills and behaviors

A key to successful organizational change is proactively planning for the change and the inevitable emotional responses that it will evoke. Emotions are a major driving force for behavior therefore care must be taken to recognize people's strengths, weaknesses, and ability to accept change. Emotional responses vary based on the size and impact of the change and may include those listed in Table 9.1.

Not everyone welcomes change, even when the change is needed. Studies have shown that resistance is all about the way those affected by a change *think* it will alter their established relationship in the organization. Resistance is compounded when people rely on second-hand information that may—or may not—be accurate.

In his widely touted essay, *Leading Change: Why Transformation Efforts Fail*, Harvard Business School Professor John P. Kotter breaks down the process of leading and creating change in an organization into eight steps. They are:

1. Establish a sense of urgency
2. Form a powerful guiding coalition
3. Create a vision
4. Communicate that vision
5. Empower others to act on the vision
6. Plan for and create short-term wins
7. Consolidate improvements and keep the momentum for change moving
8. Institutionalize the new approaches

OCM begins with a compelling reason to change—an urgent need to change—and seeks to understand the perspective of the affected parties, and why they feel the way they do. Planning efforts can then determine how best to help people understand the need for and accept the change.

Figure 9.1 illustrates that even when people initially express enthusiasm for a change, OCM activities must address the fact that over time, enthusiasm can lead

Table 9.1 Emotional responses to organizational change

Emotional responses to change	
Shock	Panic
Denial	Depression
Anger	Resignation
Guilt	Acceptance

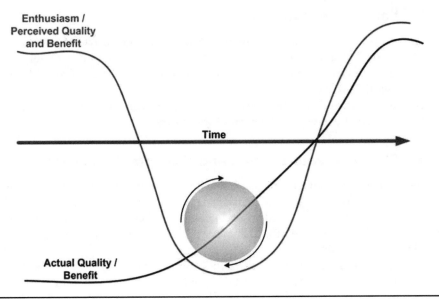

Figure 9.1   The emotions of organizational change

to confusion and frustration. Because of this, efforts must be made to keep the momentum going.

Kotter's last two steps are particularly relevant to the topic of momentum and he cautions leaders against "declaring victory too soon." Care must be taken to **institutionalize** the change, which means ensure the change is accepted as a way of doing business. In other words, ensure the change becomes "the way we do things."

People cannot be forced to change, nor can people change instantly or overnight, just because they have been directed to do so. Successful organizational change takes time and effort and must occur with people and for people, and not to people.

Keys components of a successful OCM program include:

- Change preparation
    - **Step 1:** Create a vision and promote awareness
    - **Step 2:** Identify and empower change agents
    - **Step 3:** Create a communication plan
- Motivation
    - **Step 4:** Create an incentive plan
- Education and training
    - **Step 5:** Create an education and training plan

9.1 Change Preparation

Nothing can be more frustrating than to have a project delayed due to lack of commitment. It is important to understand that a lack of commitment very often stems from the lack of a vision, or failure to continuously and consistently communication that vision.

It is the responsibility of the organization's leadership team to remain strategically focused and create a clear vision of the future.

9.1.1 Step 1: Create a Vision and Promote Awareness

While management must be engaged, this first activity speaks to the very essence of what **leadership** is all about... inspiring and motivating people to abandon old habits and embrace new ideas and goals. It is then the **management** team's responsibility to determine how to achieve goals by planning, managing, and controlling people's activities.

Leadership and management are both important but they each play a slightly different role. A frequently heard refrain is that leadership is doing the right thing and management is doing things right. The most effective leaders and managers have characteristics of both of these roles. Leaders with management skills are able to understand what it is going to take to institutionalize their vision. Managers with leadership skills are able to motivate their teams and instill in them the desire to continually improve.

Change preparation begins with management determining and coordinating the resources needed to accomplish the future state set forth by the organization's leaders. To be successful, management must accept the fact that (1) change takes time and (2) they must be prepared to answer comments and questions such as:

- Here we go again
- This is a waste of time
- Haven't we tried this before?
- Why are we fixing something that isn't broken?
- How soon is this going to happen?
- How long is this going to take?
- How is this going to affect me?
- What's in it for me?

These comments and questions are inevitable and must be answered quickly and honestly or resistance will settle in. Simply put, management must communicate the realities of the current state and put forth a business case for change. Organizations change for two primary reasons:

1. To get better or to be the best
2. To deal with painful circumstances such as a downturn in the economy, a loss of revenue, or poor performance

Management must be honest with workers about these realities and convince them that the best way to deal with those realities is through change. Having said that, management must be realistic and understand that people's ability to understand and accept change will vary, as will their willingness to participate and contribute to the change.

Table 9.2 shows workers' willingness to change in a typical organization, along with recommended management actions. Successful OCM engages the early adopters in change planning activities, assigns them responsibility for some aspect of the plan, and gives them a reason to get involved and get excited.

9.1.2 Step 2: Identify and Empower Change Agents

OCM aims to fill two common voids in a traditional project plan. They are:

- Stakeholder involvement
- Communications

Stakeholder involvement is critical because people who participate in deciding what will change and how things will change are far more likely to accept change.

> *People typically don't resist their own ideas.*

Change agents play an important role as they help people move towards change. Whether formally or informally, change agents contribute by:

- Demonstrating a willingness to embrace the new process
- Becoming knowledgeable about the new process and serving as a subject matter expert
- Giving feedback on the new process and associated procedures
- Viewing process problems as opportunities and helping to create solutions

Table 9.2 Workers' willingness to change and management actions

Willingness to change	Management action
13.5% of workers are early adopters and about 2.5% of early adopters are innovators who initiate change	Engage these forward thinkers and empower them to serve as change agents
68% of workers will change with encouragement and prove that the change is worth the pain and effort	Provide a clear vision, training, and proof of concept
16% of workers are naysayers who will view the change negatively and may never accept the change	Focus on the upper 84%

Adapted from Everett M. Rogers adoption/innovation curve.

- Leading process implementation activities for their area of the business
- Communicating process goals and influencing the way the change is perceived

9.1.3 Step 3: Create a Communication Plan

Poor or inadequate communication is one of the most common reasons that change efforts fail. It is imperative that all levels of management, all members of the project team, and all of the individuals who will be affected by a process design or improvement project send and receive timely and appropriate communications about how the project is progressing and its predicted effects.

As illustrated in Figure 9.2, communication must be continuous, consistent, and aimed at keeping all parties focused on the goals to be achieved and the desired future state. Appendix E provides a sample communication plan template.

An effective communication plan will clearly and continuously communicate:

- Why the new or improved process is needed
- The goals and objectives of the new process
- The progress and plans relative to process design and implementation activities
- Change details such as who, what, when, where, why, and how

> *Some organizations create a communication theme or "brand" that helps ensure messages are consistent and recognized as part of a greater program. A consistent theme or brand makes it possible to differentiate a program's message from all of the other communications occurring at any point in time.*

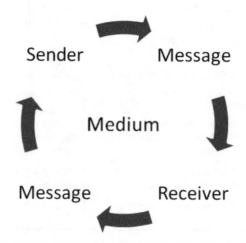

Sender   Message

Medium

Message   Receiver

Figure 9.2 On-going communications model

Communication planning must consider:

- When communications will occur and to whom
- Interests and language of the recipients
- Message to be delivered
- How the message will be delivered (i.e., the appropriate medium)
- Purpose and goal of the communication
- Who will develop the communication vehicle
- Who will approve the communication vehicle
- How to accommodate two-way communication
- How the effectiveness of communications will be measured

> *"Without credible communication, and a lot of it, the hearts and minds of the troops are never captured."*   John P. Kotter

A comprehensive, organization-wide communication plan is needed that promotes awareness and understanding of the change. The plan must also:

- Reflect the actions of leadership and management
- Describe the business benefits of the change
- Answer the question "What's in it for me?"
- Deliver messages tailored to the target audience
- Deliver timely messages
- Use simple language
- Be highly repetitive
- Have a mechanism that enables two-way communication
- Celebrate accomplishments

Touting quick wins is an important aspect of change communication as it provides the proof of concept needed to convince the majority of adopters that the concept is sound and that the change, in the end, will be worth the discomfort or pain needed to make the change.

For high-impact implementations in particular, all of the participants in process definition, design, and implementation activities must positively promote the benefits of the new or improved process and serve as an advocate during its implementation.

9.2 Motivation

It is often said that people cannot be motivated; that motivation comes from within. Job theorists have found that internal motivation requires three primary elements:

1. Meaningful work—people understand the benefits of what they do

2. A sense of autonomy—people can choose how they complete a task and so feel ownership for the result
3. Feedback—people hear how they are doing and so can improve

Other theories about motivation that must be understood include:

- If people perceive they are being treated unfairly they'll stop listening
- If basic needs aren't being met, people won't embrace a future vision
- People expect to be rewarded for their efforts
- You get whatever behavior you reward
- One-size-fits-all rewards often don't work

9.2.1 Step 4: Create an Incentive Plan

People rarely work for free and so pay is always a motivating factor. In today's work world where money cannot always be the answer, one of the things management can do is create a motivating environment that matches people's skills and needs to their work. An aspect of OCM is planning and designing motivational rewards aimed at gaining momentum and keeping it going during times of change.

Motivational rewards that are particularly important to technical workers may include those listed in Table 9.3.

9.3 Education and Training

9.3.1 Step 5: Create an Education and Training Plan

Education and training are both forms of study and learning but they serve different purposes. **Education** focuses on acquiring general knowledge and developing

Table 9.3 Important motivational rewards for technical workers

Motivational reward	Accomplished by . . .
A feeling of accomplishment	Establishing process design and improvement projects with goals, milestones, and celebrations along the way
A sense of achievement	Ensuring people are prepared and have the tools and training needed to do their work
A fair monetary system	Clearly communicating the goals of a new process and rewarding compliance
Personal and professional growth	Encouraging innovation, eliminating low value activities, and creating opportunities to grow
Training opportunities	Creating opportunities for people to develop new skills both technical and nontechnical

capabilities such as reasoning and judgment (i.e., learning to know). **Training** is practical education (i.e., learning to do). Simply put, education focuses on building the mind; training on building skills.

Education and training can occur formally in a physical or virtual classroom, or informally via a self-paced media such as e-learning. There are also hundreds of books, CDs, and podcasts—such as those listed in Appendix G—that can be used as part of a self-study program to round out your knowledge and skills.

Both education and training are required when planning projects designed to effect culture change, as is the case with process design and improvement.

In the context of ITSM, education will focus on:

- The purpose and goals of ITSM
- The benefits of ITSM
- ITSM processes
    - The purpose of each
    - How they integrate
- Where applicable, a best practices framework

Quick Tip:	Many frameworks offer introductory, or foundation courses aimed at covering these topics. These courses may be certification or non-certification courses, as dictated by an organization's goals and culture.

Education is particularly important for managers, supervisors, and individuals who are serving as change agents. Through education these individuals are able to:

- Answer questions about leadership's vision and the goals of current programs or projects
- Contribute to the attainment of goals and so enhance their own value to the organization
- Build better relationships with their staff and co-workers by encouraging two-way communication and listening to and addressing issues and concerns

Education may also include general awareness or overview classes that may be made available to all stakeholders to promote a common understanding and vocabulary.

Training focuses on the specific skills, attributes, and competencies that people need to perform a given role within a particular process or set of processes. Appendix F provides a sample training plan template. Training may include:

- Role-related responsibilities and authorities
- Related policies and procedures

- Needed technical or soft skills
- Related tools and technologies

Role-based training maps the skills that people need to their responsibilities and level of authority. The following are examples of responsibilities and skill sets that may be defined in the context of ITSM.

- ITSM responsibilities may include:
  - Defining strategy and planning
  - Management (e.g., process management)
  - Administration
  - Development
  - Implementation
- ITSM skills may include:
  - Business skills such as the ability to understand and speak the language of business
  - Soft skills such as listening and communication skills
  - Self-management skills such as stress and time management
  - Technical skills such as the skills needed to use and support technology

The most effective training programs:

- Are preceded by and integrated with education programs
- Promote awareness of why the new skills are needed
- Incorporate activities geared to both retention and application
- Provide people time to practice
- Put the practice in context (i.e., relate simulation exercises or assignments to an individual's role)

Optimally, role-based training utilizes a learner's prior experience and knowledge as a foundation for new skills.

> *ISO/IEC 20000 includes requirements relating to competence, awareness, and training. The standard states, for example, that all service management roles and responsibilities shall be defined and maintained together with the competencies required to execute them effectively. The standard also states that it is top management's responsibility to ensure workers understand the importance of their activities and how they contribute to the achievement of the service management objectives.*

Management must understand that it is unreasonable to expect people to change without management commitment in the form of resources, training, and

Table 9.4 Required management soft skills

Required management soft skills	
Coaching	Dealing with conflict
Team building	Negotiation
Listening	Delegation

support. Management support requires soft skills that individual managers may need to hone through a training program of their own such as those listed in Table 9.4.

Change is never easy and it almost always takes longer and costs more than anyone wants or expects. This is because just as with motivation, you cannot change people. They can only change themselves, and they'll only do so when they are ready. OCM provides the preparation, motivation, and education people need to see the benefits of process design and improvement activities and, ultimately, become an enthusiastic agent of change.

> *Congratulations! You have just accepted
> the role of change champion.*

The next section briefly discusses how to evaluate and select technologies that can be used to automate and enable processes.

Summary

Change is both inevitable and essential to an organization's ability to mature and grow. OCM is the process of preparing, motivating, and equipping people to meet new business challenges.

A key to successful organizational change is proactively planning for the change and the inevitable emotional responses that change will evoke. Successful organizational change takes time and effort and must occur *with* people and *for* people, and not *to* people.

Change preparation involves creating a vision and promoting awareness, identifying and empowering change agents, and creating a communication plan. Creating a vision is the responsibility of the organization's leadership. It is then management's responsibility to determine how to achieve those goals by planning, managing, and controlling people's activities. Management must be honest with workers and realistic. They must also understand that people's ability to accept change will vary, as will their willingness to participate and contribute to the change.

Successful OCM engages early adopters in change planning activities, assigns them responsibility for some aspect of the plan, and gives them a reason to get involved and get excited. Stakeholder involvement is also critical because people who participate in deciding what will change and how things will change are far less likely to resist the change.

Poor or inadequate communication is one of the most common reasons that change efforts fail. A comprehensive, organization-wide communication plan is needed that promotes awareness and understanding of the change. The plan must communicate why the change is needed, its goals and objectives, progress and plans relative to change activities, and change details such as who, what, when, where, why, and how.

It is often said that people cannot be motivated; that motivation comes from within. An aspect of OCM is planning and designing motivational rewards aimed at gaining momentum and keeping it going during times of change. Motivation rewards are particularly important to technical workers and include: a feeling of accomplishment, a sense of achievement, a fair monetary system, personal and professional growth, and training opportunities.

Education and training serve different purposes. Education focuses on building the mind. Training focuses on building skills. An education and training plan ensures both are considered, particularly when planning projects are designed to effect culture change.

Education is important for managers, supervisors, and individuals who will be serving as change agents. Education provides these individuals the ability to answer questions, contribute to the attainment of goals, and encourage two-way communication by listening to and addressing concerns. Education may also include awareness or overview classes for all stakeholders to promote a common understanding and vocabulary.

Training tends to be role-based and maps the skills that people need to their responsibilities and level of authority. Optimally, role-based training utilizes a learner's prior experience and knowledge as a foundation for new skills. The most effective training programs are preceded by and integrated with education.

Discussion Topics

- Not everyone welcomes change. Why do people resist change, even when the change is needed?
- Some workers are chronic complainers or naysayers. What positive techniques can be used to deal with naysayers?
- Developing an effective communication plan is an important and difficult aspect of organizational change. Why do efforts to communicate often fail?

Review Questions

1. What is a sign of an institutionalized change?
2. What are the three key components and five steps of an organizational change management program?
3. What are the characteristics of leadership and management?
4. What are two reasons that organizations change?
5. Why is stakeholder involvement critical when managing organizational change?
6. List four items that a communication plan must convey about a process change.
7. Internal motivation requires what three elements?
8. List five examples of motivational rewards.
9. Describe the difference between education and training.
10. Provide six examples of soft skills managers may need to hone to manage organizational change.

This book has free material available for download from the
Web Added Value™ resource center at *www.jrosspub.com*

10

IT Service Management Technologies

ITSM technologies have advanced considerably in recent years, and the available choices are staggering. Many technology vendors have integrated ITSM best practices into their tools. As a result, these technologies can be used to considerably increase the efficiency and effectiveness of your ITSM processes.

Available technologies underpin all ITSM processes and include:

- Stand-alone tools that support single processes
- ITSM suites that enable integration of several processes
- System, network, and application management technologies
- Service reporting tools and dashboards

The selection, acquisition, customization, and implementation of ITSM technology can represent a six to nine month effort, if not longer. Before evaluating tools, it is imperative to:

- Define the critical success factors for the project
- Define requirements for the new system
- Distinguish between needing a new tool and needing to refine your ITSM processes

People working in IT organizations tend to be very enamored with technology. They sometimes feel the need to have the "latest and greatest," without really taking into consideration a product's ability to adequately underpin processes, or be integrated with other available tools. Conversely, it is common for IT organizations to under-utilize tools. They acquire a software suite and use only one application, even though they could benefit from the other applications. Finally, even the best tools will not be used if their purpose and benefits have not been defined and explained. People will just work around the tools or use them in a limited fashion.

10.1 Evaluating and Selecting Technologies*

This section provides a step-by-step overview of a technology selection project. This approach, or methodology, can be used to select and implement any new technology.

The seven technology selection steps we will discuss in detail are:

1. Define your goals
2. Define your technology requirements
3. Weight your technology requirements
4. Select candidate vendors
5. Evaluate the candidates
6. Evaluate the finalists
7. Make a final decision

10.1.1 Define Your Goals

The first step is to define the goals of your project and of the new system. These goals should be as specific as possible and driven by your ITSM plan or related process-specific or service improvement plans. We all know that achieving organizational change is difficult. However, commitment climbs when people can see the benefits of making a change, especially when there is a benefit to them personally (e.g., work activities are automated or their ability to communicate and collaborate is enhanced).

Involve all of the groups and departments that will, or may, use the system in the process of defining your goals and requirements. Most organizations establish a committee that remains intact until a final decision is made. Sample goals may include:

- Facilitate workflow automation
- Enable management by exception
- Establish and maintain definitive sources of data and information
- Provide data and information that facilitates service reporting and effective management decisions
- Provide the data and information needed to anticipate and prevent the occurrence and recurrence of incidents and service outages
- Enhance customer self-sufficiency
- Provide customers timely and accurate status information

---

*This section is from Knapp, *A Guide to Service Desk Concepts*, 3E. 2010, South-Western, a part of Cengage Learning, Inc. (Reproduced by permission. www.cengage.com/permissions)

Notice that these goals are measurable and therefore can be used to demonstrate a return on investment. Defining clear goals can help you cost-justify new systems, and will also enable you to communicate to vendors what you are trying to achieve. In addition to showing how their products satisfy your requirements, require that vendors demonstrate specifically how their products will help you achieve your goals.

10.1.2. Define Your Technology Requirements

Just as it is critical to define requirements before undertaking a process design or improvement initiative, it is imperative that you define high-level requirements for your new system. You can then drill down to specific feature and functionality requirements. Common pitfalls to avoid when defining requirements include:

- Requirements that are vague
- Requirements that are too specific

Requirements that are vague will add little to the selection process. Requirements that are too specific may cause you to eliminate a vendor candidate too early in the process. Technology requirements include:

- High-level requirements
- Feature and functionality requirements

Begin by defining your high-level requirements as they will help you:

- Provide a framework for the definition of your feature and function requirements
- Narrow the field of candidate vendors

Sample high-level requirements include:

- Platform
- Performance and scalability
- Intended uses such as processes to be supported
- Ease of use
- Integration capability
- Vendor stability and support

Next, drill down and define your feature and functionality requirements. Defining categories of requirements is a good place to start. Sample feature and functionality categories include the following requirements:

- Operating
- Configuration/customization
- Data/reporting
- Usability
- Process-related
- Miscellaneous

10.1.3. Weight Your Technology Requirements

Once you have defined your requirements, the next step is to weight or priori-tize your requirements. Defining everything as a "must have" requirement could extend your search as you may eliminate a very viable candidate early in the process or end up with no vendors meeting your criteria. It also implies that you expect to find the perfect system, which is rarely the case.

Quick Tip:	A good rule of thumb is to expect 80% of your requirements to be satisfied "out of the box."

A rating system, such as the one shown in Table 10.1, can be used to weight your requirements.

10.1.4. Identify Candidate Vendors

Once you have finalized your requirements, identifying candidate vendors is one of the most difficult steps in the software selection process. Hundreds of ITSM vendors offer products, and many vendors offer multiple, or a suite of products. So, where do you begin?

Begin by looking at your requirements and determining, if possible, the cat-egory of tool you should be looking at. Factors which influence what category (or tier) a product falls into include:

- Price
- Features and functionality
- Integration capability
- Ability to configure

Resources you can use to help narrow the field include:

- Conferences, expos, and technology showcases
- Trade publications (remember that articles are not always unbiased)
- The web (e.g., vendor home pages and discussion forums)
- Gartner Magic Quadrant and Forrester Wave reports

Table 10.1 Sample requirements weighting system

Weight: The weight of importance assigned to each of your requirements
1 = Not very important
2 = Somewhat important (nice to have)
3 = Important
4 = Very important
5 = Extremely important (must have)

10.1.5. Evaluate the Candidates

Evaluation techniques include:

- **Do it yourself**—some organizations simply research the candidates via the Internet and download demo versions of the product. They then use this information to determine if the product meets their requirements. Problems that may arise with this approach include:
  - Web sites may not contain the detailed information needed
  - Not all vendors offer demos
  - You may not have sufficient structure in your process to ensure you are evaluating each of the vendors using the same criteria
- **Attend a trade show**—some organizations go to a conference or vendor showcase, attend numerous vendor demonstrations, and select a product based on what they see and hear. While this may seem like a good approach, a showcase environment does not lend itself to thoughtful analysis. Problems that may arise with this approach include:
  - Conferences and vendor showcases tend to be noisy and crowded.
  - The vendors rarely have time to talk with you about a detailed set of requirements.
  - Most companies cannot afford to send all of the stakeholders involved in making the selection to a conference.
  - It's easy to get sold. Product demonstrations can be dazzling and there are some wonderful salespeople at these shows. One can get caught up in the excitement and make a spur of the moment decision.

  If you do attend a tradeshow during your vetting process, be sure to utilize the other resource available to you at the show . . . other attendees. Ask your peers about their tools, their tool selection process, and their experience working with the tools and vendors.
- **Distribute a request for information**—recommended when a more formal approach is needed.

Distribute a Request for Information

The most effective way to reduce the time required to evaluate vendors is to prepare and distribute a **request for information (RFI)**, which is a form or letter that asks for specific product information relative to a company's requirements. While often perceived as the most time consuming approach, an RFI is by far the most thorough and objective way to evaluate products. It can also reduce the time it takes to select a product as you are engaging all of the vendors at the same time, and you are placing the burden of documentation on the vendors.

> An alternative is to send a **request for proposal**, which is a form or letter that requires financial information as well as specific product information relative to a company's requirements. This technique is typically used when there is a relatively short list of vendors.

When preparing an RFI, include the following information:

- **Introduction to your company**—include information about your company, the goals of your project, and a summary of your strategy for implementing a new system. Be specific!
- **Response guidelines**—describe how, when, and to whom vendors are expected to respond.
- **Selection criteria**—spell out the criteria you will be using to select finalists. For example:
  - Thoroughness of responses to your RFI
  - System features and functionality
  - System ease of use
  - System responsiveness
  - System architecture
  - Quality of system and documentation
  - Total implementation cost
  - Vendor's qualifications, experience, and references
  - Vendor's ability to consistently deliver quality service and support (pre and post-sale)
    - What frameworks or standards does the vendor use to ensure the quality of its services?
    - How does the vendor ensure its employees have the required knowledge and skills; what certifications do employees hold?
  - Vendor stability
  - Vendor's ability to provide training

- **Vendor and product information**—ask the vendor to spell out how their company and product satisfies your requirements. Make sure you ask specific questions, and where possible, ask questions that require a "yes" or "no" answer. This will make it easier for you to score the products.
- **Solution costs**—instruct the vendors to provide the total cost of the proposed solution and to break the costs down so that you can pick and choose options such as:
  - Base or core product

- o Adding additional users
- o Add-on modules (e.g., knowledge base, inventory management, email, report writer, development tools, etc.)
- o Annual maintenance
- o Upgrade and support fees (if not included in annual maintenance)
- o Training services
- o Consulting services (e.g., implementation, database conversion, and system design and customization assistance)
- **Contractual agreements**—require that vendors include a copy of the standard software license agreement and software product maintenance agreement for the proposed products.
- **References**—require that vendors provide at least three references.

Quick Tip:	Some vendors offer RFI forms which are biased to their products. Government RFIs can also be found on the Internet. Use these various forms as input when creating your own RFI document.

Quick Tip:	So that you can be sure you are comparing apples to apples, require that all vendor responses are based upon the currently available production version/release of their system, not a future release. Allow them to include a separate section in their response where they tell you about their next release. Indicate that vendors must clearly state when a supporting product or add-on module is required to address your requirement.

Scoring Responses

Regardless of the approach you choose to select vendors and solicit their responses, use a scoring system such as the example provided in Table 10.2 to determine how each of the candidate vendors satisfy your requirements.

Scoring formula: **Score = Weight x Rate**

Table 10.2 Sample requirements rating system

Rate: Each product's ability to satisfy your requirements	
1 = Poor	Requirement is not satisfied
2 = Fair	Borderline implementation of requirement (e.g., there is a workaround)
3 = Good	Requirement is satisfied through an add-on module or is partially satisfied
4 = Very good	Requirement is satisfied out-of-the-box
5 = Excellent	Requirement is fully satisfied out-of-the-box with additional capability

Table 10.3 Sample requirements evaluation matrix

Req #	Requirement	Weight	Vendor 1 R / S	Vendor 2 R / S	Vendor 3 R / S	Vendor 4 R / S	Vendor 5 R / S
Operating requirements							
1	Client platform	5	4 / 20	5 / 25	4 / 20	4 / 20	3 / 15
2	Server platform	5	5 / 25	5 / 25	3 / 15	4 / 20	4 / 20
3	Database	5	4 / 20	4 / 20	3 / 15	4 / 20	4 / 20
Total score			65	70	50	60	55

An evaluation matrix such as the one shown in Table 10.3 makes it easy to collect and compare vendor scores.

10.1.6. Evaluate the Finalists

If you have selected your candidates carefully, you may find the scores are very close. The ITSM tools market place is extremely competitive, and, without the benefit of rigorous hands-on testing, scores cannot be considered 100% accurate. However, evaluating the candidates (discussed in the previous step) should have helped you to further narrow the field.

This final evaluation involves taking the top two vendors (i.e., the two vendors that have the highest scores) and performing the following additional steps:

- Have finalists come to your company and demonstrate their offerings
- Contact finalists' references
- If possible, visit other sites that are using the finalists' products
- Install and conduct hands-on testing of evaluation copies of the finalists' products

Vendor Demonstrations

Have the two finalists come to you to present information about their company and demonstrate their system to your software selection committee.

To ensure the demonstrations add value to the selection process:

- Give each finalist a specified period of time
- Provide finalists a list of key topics to be covered
- Provide ample time for a question and answer session
- Make sure that all of the stakeholders that will be using the system have representatives at the demonstrations
- Ensure that individuals such as technical specialists who can further assess the vendors' conformance to your technical requirements attend as well

If possible, have the vendors demonstrate on the same day or on back-to-back days so that attendees won't forget what they saw from one demonstration to the next. Also, having the same representatives attend each of the demonstrations will enable a more consistent and fair comparison.

Following each demonstration, distribute a vendor evaluation form and have all of the attendees evaluate the products that were demonstrated.

Vendor References

Contact at least three references provided by the vendors and, if possible, visit sites where the product has been implemented. How many sites you visit will depend on the amount of time you can allocate to these visits and the budget you have available to travel. Ask the vendor for a reference who was dissatisfied, and they "won" back. This will allow you to discuss the vendor's approach to conflict resolution and commitment to customer satisfaction.

Quick Tip:	When asking for references, indicate that you want to contact companies that are using the same version/release of the proposed product, as well as any supporting products or add-on modules.

10.1.7 Make a Final Decision

When you have completed all of the steps outlined above, assemble and review the results of your evaluation efforts, and make a final decision. If you have taken your time, worked diligently to protect the integrity of the selection process, and documented your efforts along the way, the final decision should be an easy one.

Before you move on to the implementation phase, prepare a **technology selection report** that describes the selection process you followed and how the final decision was made. Include the following:

- **Introduction**—describe the goals of your project
- **Summary of requirements**—provide a brief, executive overview of your requirements
- **Evaluation methodology**—describe the process you used to select and evaluate the candidates and how you made the final decision
- **Next steps**—provide a high-level overview of the steps required to implement the solution
- **Appendices**—include all of the results you collected (e.g., your evaluation matrix, the completed questionnaires, the notes from your meetings with references, and so forth)

The implementation of a product goes much more smoothly when users are confident that care was taken to select the best possible solution.

10.2 Planning and Managing a Successful Implementation

Planning and managing a successful ITSM technology implementation is really no different than any other technology implementation. Your plan or "roadmap" represents the steps that must be taken to ensure that your project runs smoothly and achieves its stated goals. In addition to a detailed plan, strong leadership and proper staffing are extremely important components of a successful implementation. Poorly managed, and improperly staffed, even the best laid plans will fail.

With any major project there are two main factors that will dictate the duration of the project: (1) the tasks to be performed, including the level of detail and quality required, and (2) the required skill and availability of the resources performing the tasks.

The greatest variables affecting the duration of your project will be the system design and development activities. Complex interfaces and modifications can significantly alter the amount of development effort required. By selecting a tool that meets your requirements and "keeping it simple" initially, you can get your system up and running more quickly. Plan ahead and dedicate resources to fine-tuning activities and system enhancements once the system's capabilities and limitations are more fully understood.

Summary

ITSM technologies have advanced considerably in recent years and the available choices are staggering. Available technologies underpin all ITSM processes and include: stand-alone tools that support single processes, suites that enable integration of several processes, system, network, and application management technologies, and service reporting tools and dashboards.

The selection, acquisition, customization, and implementation of ITSM technology can represent a six to nine month effort, if not longer. Before evaluating tools, it is imperative to: define the critical success factors for the project, define requirements for the new system, and distinguish between needing a new tool and needing to refine your ITSM processes.

A methodical, seven step approach can be used to select and implement any new technology. The first step is to define the goals of your project and the new system. Goals should be measureable so they can be used to demonstrate a return on investment. Clear goals also enable you to communicate to vendors what you are trying to achieve.

The next steps involve defining high-level requirements for the new system, and then drilling down to specific feature and functionality requirements. A rating system can then be used to weight or prioritize the requirements.

Identifying candidate vendors is a difficult step. Begin by using your requirements to determine the category of tool being considered. Factors that influence what category or tier a product falls into include price, features and functionality, integration capability, and ability to configure.

Candidate evaluation techniques include: do it yourself, attend a tradeshow, and distribute an RFI. An RFI is the most thorough and objective way to evaluate products. It can also take less time because it engages all vendors at the same time and it places the burden of documentation on the vendor.

Use a scoring system to determine how each candidate vendor rates relative to your requirements. An evaluation matrix makes it easy to collect and compare vendor scores. Further evaluate the top two vendors by: having the vendors conduct demonstrations, contacting the vendors' references and conducting site visits, and installing and conducting hands-on testing.

Assemble and use the results of your evaluation efforts to make a final decision. Prepare a technology selection report that describes the selection process and how the final decision was made. Also prepare an implementation plan that describes the steps that must be taken to ensure your project runs smoothly and achieves its stated goals.

Strong leadership and proper staffing are extremely important components of a successful implementation. Plan ahead and dedicate resources to fine-tuning activities and system enhancements once the system's capabilities and limitations are more fully understood.

Discussion Topics

- People often encourage the use of their favorite system or a system they've used before. Why is important to use a methodical approach when selecting technology?
- Some vendors offer "turnkey" solutions and the promise of a swift implementation. What are the dangers of such an approach?
- A technology implementation doesn't end when the software is installed. What resources are required to maintain and support technology on an ongoing basis?

Review Questions

1. What is the first step of a technology selection project?
2. List and briefly describe the two common pitfalls to avoid when defining technology requirements.
3. Why is it not a good idea to define all of your requirements as "must have"?
4. What is a good first step when identifying candidate vendors?

5. What is the most effective way to reduce the time required to evaluate vendors? Explain your answer.
6. List three tips that can help ensure you receive proper vendor and product information in an RFI.
7. True or false. Use a scoring system to determine how each of the candidate vendors satisfies your requirements only if you are evaluating three or more vendors. Explain your answer.
8. After you have scored the various vendor responses to your RFI, what should you do next?
9. Why is it a good idea to have the finalists demonstrate their products on the same day or on back-to-back days?
10. What are three essential components for a successful ITSM technology implementation?

This book has free material available for download from the
Web Added Value™ resource center at *www.jrosspub.com*

Appendix A

Sample Process Definition Document

INFORMATION TECHNOLOGY SERVICES
INCIDENT MANAGEMENT
PROCESS DEFINITION DOCUMENT

Prepared by:
Incident Management Process Improvement Team

Prepared for:
Information Technology Services

Version 1.0
September 26, 2011

Introduction

The purpose of this document is to describe the incident management process sanctioned by the Information Technology Services (ITS) organization. Incident management is one of several key processes that enable ITS to deliver the highest quality customer support possible. Other key processes that integrate closely with incident management include:

- Problem management
- Change management
- Request fulfillment
- Service asset and configuration management
- Service level management

1.0 High-Level Process Definition

Incident management is the process of tracking and resolving incidents in a manner that satisfies the service level agreements (SLAs) between ITS and its customers. The objective of incident management is to minimize the impact of incidents that affect the services defined as within the scope of the SLAs. Goals include providing information about the status of reported incidents, maintaining a history of incidents and solutions for prevention and re-use and maximizing the availability of production services.

The components of a successful management system are:

- **People:** The individuals and teams who support customers by performing processes
- **Processes:** Interrelated work activities that take a set of specific *inputs* and produce a set of specific *outputs* that are of value to a customer
- **Technology:** The tools and technologies people use to do their work
- **Information:** The data and information people need to do their work, measure process efficiency and effectiveness, and identify improvement opportunities

This document focuses on the people, process, and information components and is designed to show responsibility for specific tasks as an incident moves from recognition to resolution. It is acknowledged that at times these activities may occur very quickly, even simultaneously. Although technology is not a focus of this document, the process refers to the ITS incident management system (IMS) as the central source of information on the status of all incidents.

This document will be reviewed annually, revised as needed, and approved by representative ITS associates who are stakeholders in the incident management process.

Appendix A provides a document control sheet.

Appendix B provides a list of process improvement team (PIT) members.

A glossary of terms is provided at the end of this document.

Throughout this document, flowcharts present an overview and more detailed views of this process. The symbols used to develop these flowcharts include:

Flowchart Legend:

Start	Process starting point
(circle)	Off page connector
(rectangle)	Single task or operation
(diamond)	Decision—used in conjunction with result arrows
(predefined process)	Predefined process (represents another process that provides input or receives output from the current process)
(parallelogram)	Information required to complete a task
Yes ——— No ——▶	Yes and no result arrows
Stop	Process termination point

2.0 Roles and Responsibilities

Described in this section are the roles and responsibilities of incident management process suppliers and customers.

Role	Responsibilities
Customer	A purchaser or consumer of ITS's support services.
Service Desk Analyst (SDA)	A service desk associate who works directly with customers, responds to contacts, solves incidents, and operates with known solutions. SDAs initially provide level one (see below) support and serve as incident owner (see below) in the event an incident must be escalated.
Customer Engineer (CE)	An ITS associate who is dispatched to provide on-site support.
Incident Owner	The SDA who accepts responsibility for proactively ensuring that an incident is resolved and the customer is satisfied. Specifically, the incident owner: <ul><li>Can provide and is aware of the current status:<ul><li>○ Who is working on the incident?</li><li>○ Where is the incident in the process?</li></ul></li><li>When possible identifies related incidents.</li><li>Ensures that incidents are correctly assigned.</li><li>Ensures that appropriate notification activities occur at the time an incident is reported, in conjunction with pre-defined escalation guidelines, and at the time an incident is resolved.</li><li>Prior to closing an incident:<ul><li>○ Ensures all associates involved in incident solving activities have documented their activities in accordance with pre-defined standards.</li><li>○ Ensures the customer is satisfied with the resolution.</li></ul></li></ul>

Roles	Responsibilities
Level one	The initial point of contact within ITS when an incident is recognized.

- Gathers data and records the incident.
- Determines the probable incident source.
- Engages needed resources in incident resolution activities.
- Resolves incidents when possible using available tools and procedures.
- Documents the resolution.
- Negotiates a priority with the customer.
- Documents current status and resolution steps attempted or completed.
- Escalates to level two as needed.
- Assumes incident ownership.

Level two	A group that resolves incidents beyond the scope or authority of level one.

- Provides level one a function-oriented way to obtain service.
- Acknowledges assignments from level one or other level two functions; assigns the best qualified individual.
- Reviews data provided by level one or other level two functions; gathers additional data as needed.
- Engages resources as needed in incident solving activities.
- Communicates incident status to the incident owner.
- Requests incident reassignment from the incident owner when required (e.g., following analysis that results in the identification of a different probable incident source or based upon newly received information).
- Resolves incidents related to their group's particular area of expertise in a timeframe in keeping with the incident's priority.
- Documents the resolution.
- Documents current status and resolution steps attempted or completed.
- Escalates to level three when needed.

Roles	Responsibilities
Level three	A group that resolves complex incidents that are beyond the scope of level two; may involve multiple technical areas, third party vendors, or consultants. Level three:

- Provides level two a function-oriented way to obtain service.
- May be a single group or a cross-functional team brought together by level two and/or the incident owner.
- Acknowledges assignments from level two; assigns the best qualified individual. Cross-functional teams designate a facilitator to oversee this activity.
- Reviews data provided by the incident owner, from level one and level two; gathers additional data as needed.
- Engages needed resources in incident solving activities.
- Oversees resolution activities in the event an external (e.g., third party) supplier is engaged.
- Communicates incident status to the incident owner and level two.
- Resolves incidents that cross multiple technical areas or involve a third party vendor or consultant.
- Documents current status and resolution steps attempted or completed.

Note: A function-oriented approach places responsibility for ensuring individuals are available to participate in the incident management process within each functional area as opposed to within the service desk. Rather than assigning incidents to individuals, the service desk assigns incidents to a functional area. The functional area determines the individual best qualified to resolve the incident.

3.0 The Incident Management Process

Process Owner

Information Technology Services Director

Boundaries/Triggers

Start: Identification of a technology-related incident or question.
Stop: Verification that normal processing resumes or communication that the incident relates to an unsupported system, network or product. Verification that the customer is satisfied with the resolution.

Inputs

1. Technology-related incident or question
2. Telephone, fax, e-mail, direct IMS access, access via the Web, and automation
3. Incident management and resolution tools
4. Priority codes[1]
5. Target escalation/resolution time guidelines

Suppliers

- ITS customers
- Level one functions (i.e., the ITS Service Desk)
- Level two functions (e.g., Application Desktop Services, Network Services, Field Support Services)
- Level three functions (e.g., development teams, third-party vendors)

Activities

1. Acknowledge and record incident
2. Isolate and diagnose incident
3. Escalate and monitor incident
4. Attempt/verify resolution
5. Close incident

Outputs

1. Restoration of normal operations
2. When applicable, customer is notified that they are not entitled to support
3. Incident record

---

[1]Priority code definitions are provided in Appendix C

Customers

- External customers that are utilizing ITS's support services
- Internal ITS associates that provide ITS's support services

Metrics

- Customer satisfaction with the process (e.g., reporting, logging, status accounting, resolution)
- Supplier satisfaction with the process (e.g., information exchanged, knowledge transferred, timeliness of responses, etc.)
- Resolution efficiency (e.g., average time to resolve)
- Resolution effectiveness (e.g., positive trend analysis results, a low percentage of reopened or recurring incidents)

Note: The metrics presented throughout this document represent standard measures designed to gauge the efficiency and effectiveness of this process. It is expected that additional metrics and ad-hoc reports will be required and created as needed.

The following flowchart presents an overview of the incident management process.

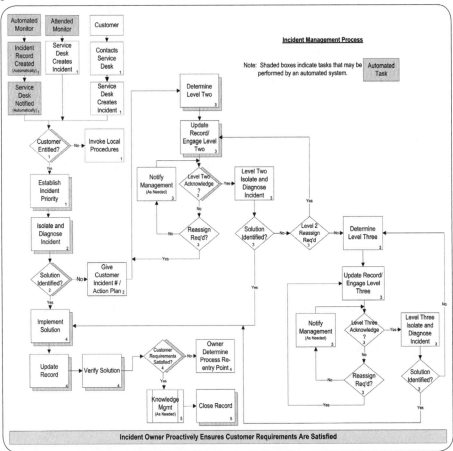

Flowcharts are included that provide more detailed views of the following sub-processes (which are designated via corresponding numbers on the overall flow above):

1. Acknowledge and record incident
2. Isolate and diagnose incident
3. Escalate and monitor incident
4. Attempt/verify resolution
5. Close incident

These sub-processes represent a logically grouped lower-level view of the activities performed within the incident management process.

3.1 Acknowledge and Record Incident

Description—This sub-process is triggered by recognition that an incident has occurred. Activities begin with notification to a single point and end when the incident has been logged and the customer has been provided an incident number. A priority that reflects the incident's impact and criticality to the customer's business is assigned to each incident. An incident owner is designated who will proactively ensure the customer's requirements are satisfied throughout the process.

Goals include:

1) Gathering sufficient data to identify the customer, verify the customer's entitlement, and describe and document the incident
2) Providing the customer an incident number and designating an incident owner

Inputs	Suppliers
• Telephone calls to the service desk	• Any ITS customer who has an incident or question
• E-mail messages sent to the service desk	
• Faxes sent to the service desk	• An automated monitoring system set-up to detect actionable events occurring on customer systems and produce alerts
• An incident logged in IMS by the customer	
• An automated system detects an actionable alert	
• An attendant monitoring an automated system detects an actionable alert	
• Data gathering requirements	
• Priority codes	
• Target escalation/resolution time guidelines	
Outputs	**Customers**
• An incident record that satisfies the data gathering requirements of ITS and the customer	• Level one
• A unique incident number	

Metrics

- Initial response time—to measure the duration of time between when the customer or an automated system reports an incident to the time when it is logged. For example, a performance goal may be that all e-mails are logged within 30 minutes.
- Perception of process
  - Customer is always given an incident number
- Monthly trend reports—to identify trends and monitor performance
  - Volume of incidents by customer
  - Number/percentage of unentitled incidents
  - Priority of incidents by customer
  - Volume of incidents by service, system, network, and/or product
  - Volume of incidents by call type (e.g., hardware, software)
  - Volume of incidents by incident type (e.g., incident, question, inquiry)
  - Volume of incidents by symptom
  - Volume of incidents by time of day, day of week, etc.

Flowchart

The following flowchart presents a detailed view of the **Acknowledge and Record Incident** sub-process.

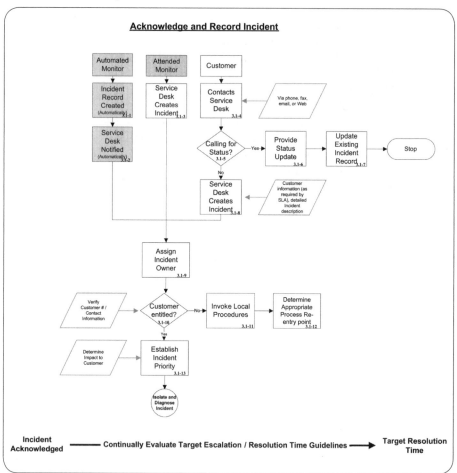

Note: Target escalation/resolution time guidelines (see Glossary) reflect ITS's SLAs with its customers and must be taken into consideration as decisions are made throughout the incident management process. These guidelines ensure that resolution activities are proceeding at a pace consistent with the priority of the incident, that the right resources are engaged at the right time, and ultimately, these guidelines enable the attainment of efficiency and effectiveness goals. Management notification guidelines are provided in Appendix D.

Activities

The following provides a narrative description of the activities associated with the **acknowledge and record incident** sub-process. The activity numbers listed below correspond to the activity numbers reflected on the flowchart on the previous page.

#	Description
3.1-1	**Incident record created (automatically):** In this scenario, an automated system is monitoring an ITS customer's system(s) and/or network. The automated system, upon detecting an actionable alert,[2] automatically creates an incident record in IMS.
3.1-2	**Service desk notified (automatically):** IMS automatically notifies the service desk that a new incident has been logged and that action is required.
3.1-3	**Service desk creates incident record:** In this scenario, the service desk is checking the console of an automated monitoring system for actionable alerts. Upon detecting an actionable alert, the SDA creates an incident record in IMS.
3.1-4	**Contacts service desk:** In this scenario, the customer contacts the service desk to report an incident by placing a telephone call, submitting a request via the web, or by sending a fax or e-mail message.
3.1-5	**Calling for status?:** The SDA determines if the customer is calling to obtain the status of an existing incident prior to creating a new incident record. Typically the customer will indicate he/she is calling for a status update.
3.1-6	**Provide status update:** If the customer is calling about an existing incident, the SDA provides a status update. The SDA determines the status by pulling up the incident record and checking its status. The SDA may also check the dispatch system or contact the Level two or Level three assignee in an effort to determine the most current status.
3.1-7	**Update existing incident record:** The SDA updates the incident and records the fact that the customer called along with any up-to-date status information obtained.
3.1-8	**Service desk creates incident record:** If the customer is not calling about an existing incident, the SDA collects required and relevant information and creates a new incident record.
3.1-9	**Assign incident owner:** Ownership is automatically assigned to the SDA who creates the incident record. Ownership may be reassigned to another SDA at any time throughout the process as needed (e.g., for shift changes, vacations, etc.).

---

[2]Not all alerts are actionable (i.e., some are informational in nature and some are warnings that do not require action at the current time).

#	Description
3.1-10	**Customer entitled?:** Before beginning to diagnose the incident, the SDA determines if the customer is entitled to support. This initial entitlement check is a "soft" check and typically occurs in the course of creating the incident (e.g., the customer provides his/her customer number).
3.1-11	**Invoke local procedures:** If the customer is not entitled to support, the SDA follows local procedures. When in doubt the SDA checks with his or her supervisor.
3.1-12	**Determine appropriate process re-entry point:** The SDA determines the appropriate process re-entry point taking into consideration factors such as local procedures and SLA terms and conditions.
3.1-13	**Establish incident priority:** If the customer is entitled to support, the SDA determines the priority of the incident. Priority is determined by listening for clues about, or by discussing with the customer, the impact of the incident on the customer's business.

3.2 Isolate and Diagnose Incident

. . . document remaining sub-processes including description, inputs, suppliers, outputs, customers, metrics, flowchart, and activities (narrative description).

Appendix A—Document Control Sheet

Document Identification	
Title	Information Technology Services Incident Management Process Definition Document
File Name	ITS IM Process Definition Document.doc
Document ID	ITSIMPDD
Document Purpose	Define the ITS incident management process including purpose, objective, goals, roles and responsibilities, process owner, boundaries/triggers, inputs, suppliers, activities, outputs, customers, metrics, and sub-processes.
Owner	Incident Management Process Owner
Author(s)	Incident Management Process Improvement Team
Status	Initial Draft
Version	1.0
Date of Draft	September 26, 2011
Feedback Due By Date	
Date Approved	
Scheduled Review Date	

Approvals			
Version	Date	Approver Name/Title	Approver Signature

Version History			
Version	Date	Change Log	Author

Distribution List		
Version	Name	Company

Appendix B—Process Improvement Team (PIT) Members

The following individuals represented their respective organizations in process design activities and by participating in the development and review of this document.

Team Member	Representing (Team)

Appendix C—Priority Code Definitions

The following priority code definitions depict the urgency of an incident. Target resolution times associated with these priorities are described in each SLA established with an ITS customer.

Priority Code	Description
Priority 1	Critical: An incident which critically impacts the customer's ability to do business. A significant number of users of the system and/or network are currently unable to perform their tasks as necessary. System and/or network is down or severely degraded.
Priority 2	Urgent: An incident which impacts the customer's ability to do business, the severity of which is significant and may be repetitive in nature. A function of the system, network, or product is impacted.
Priority 3	Routine: A minor incident which negligibly impacts the customer's ability to do business. Also includes questions and/or general consultation.

Appendix D—Management Notification Guidelines

Throughout the process there may be times when it is determined that management notification is appropriate. For example:

- The target time for resolving an incident has been or is about to be reached
- Required resources are not available to determine or implement a solution
- The customer expresses dissatisfaction

The goals of management notification are to ensure:

- Management is aware of the current status of incidents that are in an exception state
- Management is provided sufficient information to: 1) make decisions (e.g., to add more resources or re-assign incident resolution responsibilities) and 2) follow-up with the customer and/or engage other management
- Management actions are recorded in the incident record

Typically, the incident owner and the assigned line two or line three service providers will notify their respective managers. The incident owner will notify his or her manager in the event he or she is unable to obtain a response from the service provider. The incident owner's manager will then contact the assignee's manager as needed.

Glossary of Terms

DISPATCH—A term used to describe the act of engaging an ITS CE.

ESCALATE (ESCALATION)—To raise an incident from one level to another (e.g., from Level one to Level two).

INCIDENT—An event affecting the normal operation of a service or a service-related question or inquiry.

INCIDENT MANAGEMENT SYSTEM (IMS)—An automated tool used to track and manage incidents.

ISOLATE AND DIAGNOSE—To determine the probable source of an incident.

KNOWLEDGE BASE—A repository of reusable solutions identified via the incident management process. Solutions are stored in a separate file than incidents so that one solution can be used to solve many incidents.

NOTIFY (NOTIFICATION)—To engage management in the incident management process, typically on an exception basis.

PRIORITY—A consistent means of communicating the impact and criticality *to the customer's business* of reported incidents. To ensure accurate reporting, priority typically remains the same throughout the life of an incident.

PROCESS—A set of interrelated work activities that are characterized by a set of specific inputs and value-added tasks that produce a set of specific outputs.

PROCEDURE—Step-by-step instructions that describe how to perform the activities in a process.

REASSIGN—To assign incident ownership to another SDA as needed (e.g., for shift changes, vacations, etc.).

SERVICE DESK—A physical and functional approach to centralizing the resources required to provide level one customer support.

SERVICE PROVIDER—An individual and/or organization that delivers services in response to a need or demand.

SUB-PROCESS—A logically grouped lower-level view of activities performed within a process.

TARGET ESCALATION TIME—A guideline that ensures incident resolution activities are proceeding at an appropriate pace, that customers are provided timely and accurate status updates, and that management remains aware of incident resolution activities as needed.

TARGET RESOLUTION TIME—The timeframe within which it is expected an incident will be resolved. Target resolution times typically correlate to the priority of the incident and are defined in each SLA established with an ITS customer.

Appendix B

Sample Document Control Sheet

ISO/IEC 20000-1 requires the following:

- Service providers shall provide documents and records to ensure effective planning, operation and control of service management including:
  - Policies and plans
  - Service level agreements
  - Processes
  - Procedures
- Procedures and responsibilities shall be established for the creation, review, approval, maintenance, disposal and control of the various types of documents and records

Documentation can be in any form or type of medium. Document control includes activities such as:

- Knowing the revision status
- Providing evidence of approval
- Protecting the document from damage
- Protecting the document from unauthorized revision

The following is a sample Document Control Sheet:

Document Identification	
Title	
File Name	
Document ID	
Document Purpose	
Owner	
Author	
Status	
Version	
Date of Draft	
Feedback Due By Date	
Date Approved	
Effective Date	
Scheduled Review Date	
Document Authorization	
Name	
Title	
Date	
Signature	

Version History			
Version	**Date**	**Change Log**	**Author**

Distribution List		
Version	**Name**	**Company**

Appendix C

Sample High-level Implementation Plan

Incident Management Process/System High-Level Implementation Plan								
ID	TASK NAME	% COMP	STATUS	EST START DATE	ACTUAL START DATE	ACTUAL END DATE	ASGN	DELIVERABLES
100	PROJECT MANAGEMENT							Implementation Task Plan
110	Create Task Plan							Implementation Task Plan
120	Define Project Objectives/Scope (Scope - who, what, when)							Project Objectives Document
130	Select Project Leader & Team							Team Roles & Responsibilities
140	Prepare/Present Project Kick-Off							Meeting Agenda/ Minutes
150	Obtain Commitment to Proceed							Agreement to Proceed
160	Develop Communication Plan							Communication Plan
170	Ongoing Project Management							Bi-weekly Status Reports/Updated Implementation Task Plan
180	Ongoing Communication							Updated Communication Plan
200	BEGIN PROCESS IMPLEMENTATION							
210	Publish Final Process Definition Document							Process Definition Report

220	Determine Needed/Document Procedures and Work Instructions	Process-Related Procedures and Work Instructions
230	Develop Process Education Materials	Process Education Materials
240	Submit for Review	
250	Revise as Needed	Final Process Education Materials
260	Schedule Process Education	
270	Conduct Process Education—Core Process Implementation Team	
280	Conduct Process Education—IT Management	
290	Conduct Process Education—IT Staff	
300	CONDUCT SOFTWARE EVALUATION (As Needed)	Software Selection Report
310	Define Goals	Documented Project Goals
320	Define/Weight Requirements	Request for Information (inc. project goals and Requirements Matrix)
330	Select Candidates	Vendor Contact List

Incident Management Process/System High-Level Implementation Plan

ID	TASK NAME	% COMP	STATUS	EST START DATE	ACTUAL START DATE	ACTUAL END DATE	ASGN	DELIVERABLES
340	Evaluate Candidates							Completed Evaluation Matrix
350	Evaluate Finalists							Software Selection Report
350.1	Conduct Demonstrations							Completed Evaluation Forms
350.2	Conduct Hands-On Testing							Complete Requirements Checklists
350.3	Contact Vendor References							Complete Questionnaires
350.4	Review Demo/Testing/Reference Results							
360	Select Product							Product Recommendation
360.1	Schedule Site Visit for Selected Product							
360.2	Visit Site							Completed Reference Questionnaire
370	Prepare and Present Recommendation to Management							Recommendation Presentation/Report
380	Finalize Software Selection							Final Software Selection Report

		Signed Contract(s)
390	Negotiate Purchase	
400	DESIGN MANAGEMENT SYSTEM	System Design Document
410	Design/Document Mgmt System Configuration/Modifications	
410.1	Identify/Design Required Changes (if any) to Application Flow	
410.2	Identify/Design Required Changes (if any) to Screens/Fields	
410.3	Identify/Design Required Changes (if any) to Interfaces	
410.4	Identify/Design Required Changes (if any) to Reports	
420	Prepare System Design Document	System Design Document
430	Submit for Review/Approval	
440	Revise Design Document as Needed	Final System Design Document
500	CONVERSION PLANNING	
510	Define Conversion Approach (i.e., what (if any) data will be converted/map to fields in new system) - Consider relevancy and cleanliness of existing data	Conversion Plan
520	Determine Conversion Process (i.e., how the conversion will be performed)	

Incident Management Process/System High-Level Implementation Plan

ID	TASK NAME	% COMP	STATUS	EST START DATE	ACTUAL START DATE	ACTUAL END DATE	ASGN	DELIVERABLES
530	Define Conversion Resource Requirements							
540	Develop Conversion Plan							Conversion Plan
550	Submit for Review/Approval							
560	Revise Conversion Plan as Needed							Final Conversion Plan
600	DEVELOP TRAINING PROGRAM							Training Plan
610	Determine Training Needs (consider system administration, database administration, system and report development and customization, and end-user requirements)							
620	Determine How Training Will be Provided (i.e., by vendor, in-house)							
630	Determine and Document Training Facility Requirements							
640	Develop Training Plan (which reflects needs, how training will be provided, facility requirements and a schedule).							Training Plan
650	Submit for Review/Approval							
660	Revise Training Plan as Needed							Final Training Plan

#	Task					Deliverable
670	Schedule Training Facilities					
680	Begin Executing Training Plan (e.g., the System Administrator may want to attend training prior to installing the software)					
700	HARDWARE/SOFTWARE INSTALLATION					Hardware/Software Installation Plan
710	Determine and Document Hardware/Software Requirements as Needed to Support System (including client, server, database, network)					
720	Prepare Purchase Order(s)/Obtain Required Approvals					Approved Purchase Order(s)
730	Order Hardware/Software					
740	Prepare Hardware/Software Installation Plan					Hardware/Software Installation Plan
750	Execute Hardware/Software Installation Plan					
800	DEVELOP SYSTEM					
810	Prepare System Environment					System Environment(s)
810.1	Establish Test Environment					Test Environment

	Incident Management Process/System High-Level Implementation Plan							
ID	TASK NAME	% COMP	STATUS	EST START DATE	ACTUAL START DATE	ACTUAL END DATE	ASGN	DELIVERABLES
810.2	Establish Training Environment (typically the same Application level as the production environment but with its own database)							Training Environment
810.3	Establish Production Environment							Production Environment
820	USER PROCEDURES & TRAINING							Training Materials
820.1	Develop Procedures							Procedures Guide
820.2	Develop/Refine Training Materials (including System Users Guide, Quick Reference Card, and exercises that span the life cycle of an Incident)							Training Materials
830	PRODUCT CUSTOMIZATION							
830.1	Configure Product (e.g., Setup security accounts, create user profiles, etc.)							Configured Product
830.2	Customize Product Using System Design Document (i.e., modify screens/fields)							Customized Product
830.3	Develop/Customize Reports							Customized Reports
830.4	Develop/Customize Interfaces							Customized Interfaces

						System Documentation
830.5	Prepare System Document					
840	TESTING					
840.1	Develop System Test Plan					System Test Plan
840.2	Prepare Test Data					
840.3.1	Conduct Unit Testing					Incident Log
840.3.2	Resolve Incidents Identified During Unit Testing					
830.3.3	Re-Test as Needed					Updated Incident Log
840.4.1	Perform Integration Test					Incident Log
840.4.2	Resolve Incidents Identified During Integration Test					
840.4.3	Re-Test as Needed					Updated Incident Log
840.5.1	Perform User Acceptance & Stress Test					Incident Log
840.5.2	Resolve Incidents Identified During User Acceptance & Stress Test					
840.5.3	Re-Test as Needed					Updated Incident Log
850	CONVERSION PREPARATION					
850.1	Develop Conversion Programs					Conversion Programs
860	PRODUCTION TURNOVER					
860.1	Prepare Documentation Required for Production Turnover					Turnover Package
860.2	Setup Backup Programs and Provide for Disaster Recovery					Backup/Recovery Programs in Place

| | Incident Management Process/System High-Level Implementation Plan | | | | | | | |
ID	TASK NAME	% COMP	STATUS	EST START DATE	ACTUAL START DATE	ACTUAL END DATE	ASGN	DELIVERABLES
860.3	Execute Turnover to Production							Approved Turnover Package
900	CONDUCT TRAINING							
910	Setup Training Facility (e.g., install the client software, make sure the necessary security has been setup on the system)							Training Facility Ready
920	Conduct User Training							User Training
930	Clean-up the Training System (i.e., remove the client software from the PCs in the training facility)							Training Facility Restored
1000	IMPLEMENT SYSTEM							
1010	Initialize & Tune Production Environment (i.e., verify production database is empty and optimally sized and tuned)							Production Environment Ready
1020	CONVERT DATA							
1020.1	Freeze and Secure the Existing Production Environment (to ensure no additional records are added)							

#	Task						Output
1020.2	Create Conversion Files						Conversion Files
1020.3	Purify Conversion Files						Clean Conversion Files
1020.4	Verify Conversion Files are Clean						
1020.5	Note Input Count						Input Count
1020.6	Convert Files						Output Count
1020.7	Verify the Results (i.e., verify output count matches input count)						Verified Results
1020.8	Resolve Any Conversion Incidents						Conversion Status Report
1030	Complete System Implementation						Go Live!
1040	MONITOR IMPLEMENTATION						
1040.1	Monitor System						Incident Log
1040.2	Monitor Processes/Procedures						Incident Log
1040.3	Record/Resolve Incidents						Updated Incident Log
1500	**POST IMPLEMENTATION REVIEW**						
1510	Perform 30 Day Follow Up Review						
1510.1	Review Objective Attainment						
1510.2	Review System & Process Performance						
1510.3	Solicit Feedback from Users						
1510.4	Document Review Results						Implementation Review Results

	Incident Management Process/System High-Level Implementation Plan							
ID	TASK NAME	% COMP	STATUS	EST START DATE	ACTUAL START DATE	ACTUAL END DATE	ASGN	DELIVERABLES
1520	Fine-tune System/Processes							Fine-tuned System/ Processes
1530	Document Future Enhancements							Include in Project Completion Report
1540	Prepare Project Completion Report							Incident Completion Report

Appendix D

Sample Key Performance Indicators

Process Group	Process	Effectiveness	Efficiency
Service Delivery	Service Level Management	• Increase in agreed service level requirements • Increase in achieved SLA targets • Increase in accurate service catalog entries	• Increase in SLA reviews conducted on time • Increase in aligned OLAs and contracts • Increase in monitoring and reporting of SLA targets
	Capacity Management	• Decrease in capacity-related incidents • Increase in accurate capacity/cost forecasts • Increase in timely capacity upgrades	• Decrease in emergency capacity purchases • Increase of performance monitoring and reporting • Increase of change impact analyses related to capacity
	Service Availability and Continuity Management	• Increase in end-to-end service availability • Increase in identified and managed risks • Decrease in the cost of unavailability	• Increase in testing after major changes • Decrease in time to perform risk analyses • Increased accuracy of the continuity plans
	Information Security Management	• Increase in conformance to security policies • Increase in risk identification and management • Decrease in security incidents	• Decrease in time to detect security incidents • Increase in security monitoring and reporting • Increase in change impact analyses related to security
	Budgeting and Accounting for IT Services	• Increase in accuracy of budgets and costs • Increase in number of costed services • Increase in fair allocation of indirect costs	• Decreased time to prepare accurate budgets • Decrease in time needed to cost services • Increase in monitoring and reporting costs against budget

	Service Reporting	• Increase in timely and accurate reports • Increase in management use of service reports	• Decrease in time to produce meaningful reports • Increase in number of clearly described reports
Control Processes	Change Management	• Decrease in change-related incidents • Decrease in unauthorized changes • Decrease in backed-out changes	• Decrease in time to process requests for change • Decrease in emergency changes • Increase in post-implementation reviews
	Configuration Management	• Increase in service quality from accurate CI information • Increase in successfully audited CI records • Increase in CIs under change control	• Decrease in CMDB errors • Decrease in time needed to audit the CMDB • Decrease in backlog of CMDB modifications
Relationship Processes	Business Relationship Management	• Increase in customer satisfaction • Increase in satisfactory complaint resolutions • Increase in actions taken from customer satisfaction surveys	• Increase in timely service reviews • Increase in documented stakeholders and customers • Increase in assigned business relationship managers
	Supplier Management	• Increase in contracts aligned to SLAs • Decrease in breaches resulting from suppliers • Increase in satisfaction with supplier performance	• Increase in supplier performance monitoring and reports • Increase in timely contract reviews • Increase in documented lead and sub-contractor relationships

Process Group	Process	Effectiveness	Efficiency
Resolution Processes	Incident Management	• Decrease in average time to resolve incidents • Increase in incidents resolved by the service desk • Increase in customer communication	• Increase in recorded incidents • Increase in correct incident categorization and prioritization • Decrease in reopened incidents • Increase in timely management reports
	Problem Management	• Decrease in recurring incidents and problems • Increase in successful corrective changes • Increase in accurate known error information	• Decrease in time to identify root cause and error correction • Increase in problems identified through proactive activities • Decrease in number of unresolved known errors
Release Processes	Release Management	• Increase in successful and timely releases • Increase in release policy conformance • Increase in cost-effective releases	• Increase in documented testing requirements • Increase in releases with documented back out plans • Increase in pre-release training and communication

Appendix E

Sample Communication Plan

Sample Communication Plan					
Audience (Who)	Materials (What)	Project Phase (When)	Venue (Where)	Key Messages (Why)	Media (How)

Communication opportunities include
- Project status
- Executive overview
- IT management overview
- IT staff overview
- Reference cards/postcards
- Newsletter articles
- New employee orientation
- Town hall meetings
- Team meetings

Appendix F

Sample Training Plan

A high-quality, cost-effective training plan meets the needs of its target audience in an agreed upon timeframe. Factors to be reflected in the plan include:

- Target audience
- Job relevancy
- Training delivery method
- Assessment testing

Target Audience

Target audience includes all of the groups who are stakeholders in the processes or tools within the scope of a given project or time frame. A matrix can be used to identify the groups to be trained and provide information such as the number of users in each group and the location where users will be trained.

Division	Department	Total # of Staff	# of Mgrs	Training Location

Job Relevancy

Job relevancy is an important factor to be considered. When job relevancy is considered, training is developed and delivered in "competency blocks" that provide learners the knowledge and skill needed to do their work.

Training should enable executive management, management, staff, and (where applicable) suppliers to understand the role they play in the associated processes or tools. This competency-based approach allows learners to focus on the competencies needed to attain job proficiency, and also allows trainers to tailor classes to the needs of their audience.

Training sessions may include:

- Overview or high-level training for executives and managers
- Process-related training (e.g., certification training) for staff who play a primary role
- Process-related training (e.g., overview training) for staff who play a secondary role
- Process-related training (e.g., advanced certification training) for process owners, process managers and key process stakeholders
- Tool-related training (e.g., hands-on training) for management and staff
- Training for system administrators

Training Delivery Method

Delivery methods will vary based on factors such as training objectives, target audience, budget, time constraints and available technical resources. Delivery methods include:

- Instructor-lead training—provides real-time access to an expert instructor, allows for class discussion and interaction
- Computer-based training or eLearning—provides training in a cost-effective way, enables self-paced independent study
- Virtual training—provides training in a cost-effective way, includes some instructor-led training in a virtual environment combined with self-study

Course materials typically include a learner manual and study aids such as a quick reference guide. These materials should compliment associated web-based resources such as online help.

Assessment Testing

Assessment testing enables trainers to evaluate the effectiveness of the instruction and course materials being delivered to students. Assessment testing also enables trainers to continuously improve the quality of the instruction and course materials being delivered to learners.

Assessment testing techniques include:

- Certification testing
- Classroom assignments and exercises
- Real world projects

Training Plan

Training-related tasks include:

- Identify trainer(s)
- Develop training curriculum
- Develop train-the-trainer program
- Gather requirements for training facilities
- Develop training schedule
- Schedule training facilities
- Develop training materials
- Execute train-the-trainer program
- Ship training materials
- Setup training facilities
- Conduct training
- Conduct assessment testing

Appendix G

Additional Sources
of Information

This appendix provides resources for additional information about process design and improvement and IT service management. Many of these resources can be obtained through your local library or via the Web.

Books

The Basics of Process Mapping. R. Damelio. Productivity Press, 1996.

The Complete Idiot's Guide to Project Management, Second Edition. S. Baker and K. Baker. Penguin Putnam, 2000.

The Complete Idiot's Guide to Technical Writing. K. Van Laan. Alpha Books, 2001.

Continual Service Improvement (IT Infrastructure Library Series). The Stationary Office, 2007.

Dictionary of Business Terms, Fourth Edition. J. Friedman. Barrons Educational Series, Inc., 2007.

Effective Presentation Skills: A Practical Guide for Better Speaking, Third Edition. S. Mandel. Crisp Publications, 2002.

The Elements of Style. R. Struck. Coyote Canyon Press, 2007.

The Elements of Technical Writing. G. Blake and R. Bly. MacMillan, 2000.

The Essential Drucker. P. Drucker. HarperBusiness, 2001.

Frameworks for IT Management. Jan van Bon (Chief Editor), Van Haren Publishing, 1996.

Getting Started in Project Management. P. Martin and K. Tate. John Wiley & Sons, 2001.

The Handbook of Technical Writing, Ninth Edition. G. Alred. St. Martin's Press, 2008.

Implementing Service and Support Management Processes: A Practical Guide. Authors (Various), C. Higday-Kalmanowitz and S. Simpson (Editors). Van Haren Publishing, 2005.

ITIL Small-scale Implementation. S. Taylor and I. Macfarlane. The Stationary Office, 2005.

Measuring ITIL. R. Steinberg. Trafford Publishing, 2006.

Metrics for IT Service Management. Jan van Bon (Chief Editor). Van Haren Publishing, 2006.

The Portable MBA, Fourth Edition. R. Bruner and R. Freeman (Contributors), M. Eaker and R. Spekman. John Wiley & Sons, 2002.

Process Mapping, Process Improvement, and Process Management. D. Madison. Paton Press, 2005.

The Quality Toolbox. N. Tague. ASQ Quality Press, 2005.

Service Design (IT Infrastructure Library Series). The Stationary Office, 2007.

Service Operation (IT Infrastructure Library Series). The Stationary Office, 2007.

Service Strategy (IT Infrastructure Library Series). The Stationary Office, 2007.

Service Transition (IT Infrastructure Library Series). The Stationary Office, 2007.

Six Sigma for IT Management. Jan van Bon (Chief Editor). Van Haren Publishing, 2006.

Pocket Guides

Dictionary of IT Service Management Terms, Acronyms and Abbreviations based on ITIL V3

Frameworks for IT Management

ITIL V3 Key Element Guide—Service Strategy

ITIL V3 Key Element Guide—Service Design

ITIL V3 Key Element Guide—Service Transition

ITIL V3 Key Element Guide—Service Operation

ITIL V3 Key Element Guide—Continual Service Improvement

ISO/IEC 20000

IT Governance based on CobiT

IT Service CMM

IT Service Management based on ITIL V3

Microsoft Operations Framework (MOF)

Planning to Implement Service Management

Certification Bodies

The Computing Technology Industry Association (CompTIA)
(630) 678-8300
www.comptia.org

CompTIA works with experts and industry leaders from the public and private sectors, including training, academia, and government to develop broad-based, foundational exams that validate an individual's IT skill set.

ITIL Exam Institutions

www.itil-offcialsite.com/ExaminationInstitutes/ExamInstitutes.asp

ITIL-related examinations are offered by a number of accredited examination institutes (EIs). EIs work with a network of accredited training organizations (ATOs) and accredited trainers with accredited materials.

Project Management Institute (PMI)

(610) 356-4600

www.pmi.com

PMI's family of credentials supports the project management profession and its practitioners and promotes ongoing professional development.

Self-Study Programs

American Management Association (AMA)

(877) 566-9441

www.amanet.org

The AMA offers seminars in topics such as communication, customer service, finance and accounting, leadership, management, project management, and time management.

CareerTrack, Inc.

(800) 780-8476, toll-free

www.careertrack.com

CareerTrack, in partnership with Fred Pryor Seminars, offers seminars in topics such as conflict and stress management, computer skills, customer service, grammar and writing, team building, and time management.

Websites

best-management-practice.com—Official OGC web site for ITIL®
itsmfusa.org—Member-driven IT service management professional forum
isixsigma.com—Six Sigma resources
isoiec20000certification.com—Official ISO/IEC Certification web site
itpi.org—IT Process Institute—Independent research organization
microsoft.com/mof—Official MOF web site—Free download
sei.cmu.edu/cmmi—Official CMMI web site

Glossary

Term	Definition
80-20 Rule	A rule that, when related to quality improvement, states that 80% of problems usually stem from 20% of the causes; also known as the Pareto principle.
Activities	The units of work to be performed within the boundaries of a process or sub-process.
As Is Flowchart	A flowchart that shows a process as it is currently being performed.
Assessment	An evaluation undertaken to baseline an organization's strengths and weaknesses and identify and recommend process improvement opportunities, priorities, and next steps.
Audit	An examination of evidence such as documents and records to verify compliance with a law, regulation, policy, or standard.
Balanced Scorecard	A performance measurement framework that combines strategic non-financial performance measures with traditional financial metrics.
Bar Chart	A chart used to compare two or more values that fall into discrete categories.
Baseline	A starting point against which to measure the effect of process improvements.

Term	Definition
Benchmarking	The process of comparing an organization's practices and performance metrics to those of another organization—or to industry best practice and industry average metrics—in an effort to identify improvement opportunities.
Best-in-Class	A company that has achieved the highest current level of performance in a particular industry.
Best Practice	A proven way of completing a task to produce a near-optimum result.
Budgeting and Accounting	(ISO/IEC 20000) Process to budget and account for the cost of service provision.
Business Case	A report that describes the business reasons that a change is being considered, along with its associated costs, benefits, and risks.
Business-Centric Culture	Business impact is predefined and understood. Priorities are based on business impact and need.
Business Process	A set of interrelated activities that accomplish a specific business goal.
Business Process Management (BPM)	A systematic approach to improving an organization's business processes.
Business Process Reengineering (BPR)	The critical analysis and radical redesign of existing business processes to achieve breakthrough improvements in performance measures.
Business Relationship Management	(ISO/IEC 20000) Process to establish and maintain a good relationship between the service provider and the customer based on understanding the customer and their business drivers.
Capability Maturity Model® Integration (CMMI)	A process improvement approach that provides organizations with the essential elements of effective processes that ultimately improve their performance.
Capacity Management	(ISO/IEC 20000) Process that ensures the service provider has, at all times, sufficient capacity to meet the current and future agreed demands of the customer's business needs.
Cause-and-Effect Diagram	A diagram used to visually display the many potential causes for a specific problem or effect. May also be called an Ishikawa or a fishbone diagram.
Certified Process Design Engineer (CPDE)®	A qualified professional who oversees process design and improvement activities and ensures processes satisfy customer requirements.
Change Agent	An individual who helps people move towards change.
Change Management	(ISO/IEC 20000) Process to ensure all changes are assessed, approved, implemented, and reviewed in a controlled manner.

Term	Definition
Check Sheet	A structured, prepared form for collecting and analyzing data.
Closed-Ended Question	A question that prompts a short, single word answer such as "yes" or "no."
Configuration Management	(ISO/IEC 20000) Process to define and control the components of the service and infrastructure and maintain accurate configuration information.
Consensus	An opinion or position reached by all of a team's members or by a majority of its members.
Contract	A legally binding agreement between an IT service provider and an external supplier, such as a vendor, contractor, or consultant.
Control	A rule designed to ensure that an organization is operating in a manner that adheres to corporate policies and procedures. The term control is most often used in the context of governance (see IT Governance and Enterprise Governance).
Control Chart	A graph used to determine if a process is in a state of statistical control.
Control Objectives for Information and related Technology (COBIT)	An IT governance framework and supporting toolset that allows managers to bridge the gap between control requirements, technical issues, and business risks.
Core Processes	Business processes that represent an organization's core competency (e.g., manufacturing, financial services, and healthcare). These processes focus on delivering a product or service to the organization's external customers.
Cost	Also known as economy, a measure used to show the cost of the process inputs required to produce the desired outputs.
Cost Benefit Analysis	An analysis that compares the costs and benefits of two or more potential solutions.
Critical Success Factor (CSF)	A measurable characteristic that must exist for a process to be viewed as successful. Critical success factors reflect the core objectives of a process and support business goals and objectives.
Cross-Functional Map	Illustrates the flow of process activities across the major functions of an organization. Also known as a swim lane diagram.
Customer	(Process) A recipient of process output.
Customer Satisfaction	The difference between how a customer expects to be treated and how a customer perceives he or she was treated.
Customer Satisfaction Surveys	A series of questions that ask customers to provide their perception of the services being offered.
Data Analysts	Individuals who are responsible for ensuring the needed data is captured, summarized, and assembled into appropriate reports and graphs.

Term	Definition
Deming Cycle	An iterative four-step approach to incremental improvement—plan, do, check, and act (PDCA). See also PDCA Cycle.
Deming Prize	Awarded in Japan to companies that have made distinctive improvements in quality or to individuals who have made major contributions to the advancement of quality.
Direct Interviewing	A requirements gathering technique that involves meeting with and questioning customers and may include conducting focus groups.
Documentation Review and Analysis	A requirements gathering technique that involves studying relevant flow charts, procedures, forms, job responsibilities, company and departmental objectives, reports, policies, regulations, statistics, etc.
Education	Acquiring general knowledge and developing capabilities such as reasoning and judgment (i.e., learning to know).
Effectiveness	A measure used to show the capability of a process to deliver value (i.e., produce a desired output).
Efficiency	A measure used to compare the value of a process (its effectiveness) with its cost.
Enterprise Governance	A set of responsibilities and practices exercised by an organization's board and executive management team with the goal of providing strategic direction, ensuring that objectives are achieved, ascertaining that risks are managed appropriately, and verifying that the enterprise's resources are used responsibly.
Event-Driven Survey	A series of questions that ask customers for feedback on a single, recent service event, such as an incident or service request.
Facilitator	An individual who serves as a project resource and leads the process improvement team through the process design and improvement steps.
Flowchart	A detailed diagram that uses standardized symbols, interconnected with lines, to show the successive steps in a process.
Framework	A logical structure for classifying and organizing complex information.
Gap Analysis	A technique that determines the steps to be taken to move from a current state to a desired future state.
Gap Analysis Report	A formal document that summarizes the findings of a gap analysis.
Goal	A targeted result. Goals must be specific, measurable, achievable, realistic, and timely (SMART).
Handoff	A process activity that occurs when a deliverable is passed from one person or function to another.

Term	Definition
High-Level Integration Map	A process map that shows the relationships that exist between interfacing processes.
Histogram	A chart that shows the distribution of data into ranges or "bins."
HP Service Management Framework	A framework that incorporates the major IT service management frameworks and standards—including ITIL, CMMI, ISO/IEC 20000, and ISO/IEC 27001—with the HP Service Management Reference Model, which provides deep-level processes that can be leveraged during process design.
IBM Tivoli Unified Process (ITUP)	A web-based tool that provides detailed documentation of IT service management processes based on industry best practices, including ITIL best practices.
Incident Management	(ISO/IEC 20000) Process to restore agreed service to the business as soon as possible or to respond to service requests.
Information	The data and information people need to do their work, measure process efficiency and effectiveness, and identify improvement opportunities.
Information Security Management	(ISO/IEC 20000) Process to manage information security effectively within all service activities.
Information Technology Infrastructure Library® (ITIL®)	A set of best practice guidance drawn from public and private sectors worldwide that describes a systematic and professional approach to the management of IT services.
Institutionalize	(Organizational Change Management) Ensuring a change is accepted as a way of doing business.
Intangible Benefit	A benefit that cannot be measured precisely.
International Organization for Standardization (ISO)	The world's largest developer and publisher of international standards.
Ishikawa Diagram	See cause-and-effect diagram.
ISO 9000	A set of universal standards for a Quality Management System.
ISO/IEC 15504	An international standard for IT process assessment that is most commonly used to assess the maturity of software development processes. Formerly known as SPICE (Software Process Improvement and Capability dEtermination.
ISO/IEC 20000	An international standard that promotes the adoption of an integrated process approach to effectively deliver managed services to meet the business and customer requirements.
ISO/IEC 20000-1	The formal Specification that defines the requirements—"shalls"—for an organization to deliver managed services of an acceptable quality for its customers.

Term	Definition
ISO/IEC 20000-2	The Code of Practice that describes best practices—"shoulds"—for service management processes within the scope of ISO/IEC 20000-1.
IT-Centric Culture	Little understanding of business impact exists and priorities are based on the pain being experienced by IT.
IT Governance	The leadership and organizational structures and processes that ensure that the organization's information technology sustains and extends the organization's strategies and objectives. IT governance is an integral part of enterprise governance.
IT Infrastructure Library® (ITIL®)	See Information Technology Infrastructure Library® (ITIL®).
ITIL® Process Maturity Framework (PMF)	A framework that can be used to assess or measure the maturity of IT service management processes.
IT Service Management (ITSM)	An integrated process approach that enables an IT organization to deliver services that meet business and customer requirements.
IT Steering Group (ISG)	A formal group of senior representatives from both the business and IT who are responsible for ensuring that business and IT strategies and plans are closely aligned.
Kaizen	The Japanese word for continuing improvement involving every-one, managers and workers alike.
Key Performance Indicator (KPI)	A key metric used to manage a process. Key performance indicators underpin critical success factors.
Leadership	Inspiring and motivating people to abandon old habits and embrace new ideas and goals. See also Management.
Leading Question	A question phrased in a way that a specific answer is expected.
Lean Six Sigma	A methodology that combines the concepts of Lean Manufacturing and Six Sigma. Lean Manufacturing focuses on removing *waste* and improving the flow of processes and pro-cedures. Six Sigma focuses on reducing *defects* by measuring standard deviations from an expected norm.
Malcolm Baldrige National Quality Award	Established in 1987 to recognize U.S. organizations for their achievements in quality and business performance, and to raise awareness about the importance of quality and performance excellence as a competitive edge.
Malcolm Baldrige Criteria for Performance Excellence	A framework of management practices that organizations can use to measure and improve their overall performance. The cat-egories that make up the award criteria for the Malcolm Baldrige National Quality Award are: leadership, strategic planning, customer and market focus, information and analysis, human resource focus, process management, and business results.

Term	Definition
Management	Determining how to achieve goals [set forth by leaders] by planning, managing, and controlling people's activities. See also Leadership.
Management Planning Committee	A team of individuals—overseen by a project sponsor—who participate in high-level goal and scope setting activities, typically in the case of large projects.
Metric	A performance measure.
Metrics Program	A measurement framework that describes the metrics needed to achieve business goals, how to collect them, and how to use them to continually improve performance. Examples of metrics programs include the Balanced Scorecard and Results that Matter approaches.
Microsoft® Operations Framework (MOF)	A framework that consists of integrated best practices, principles, and activities that provide comprehensive guidelines for achieving reliability for IT solutions and services.
Objective	An intended result (i.e., a purpose).
Open-Ended Question	A question that requires a greater answer than a single word or two.
Operational Level Agreement (OLA)	An agreement between an IT service provider and another part of the same organization.
Organizational Change Management (OCM)	The process of preparing, motivating, and equipping people to meet new business challenges.
Overall Satisfaction Survey	A series of questions that ask customers for feedback about all of their interactions with IT during a certain period of time.
Pareto Chart	A chart that shows the cumulative frequency of values plotted in a descending order.
Pareto Principle	A principle that, when related to quality improvement, states that 80% of problems usually stem from 20% of the causes; also known as the 80-20 Rule.
PDCA Cycle	An iterative four-step approach to incremental improvement—plan, do, check, and act (PDCA). See also Deming Cycle.
People	The individuals and teams who support customers by performing processes.
People-Dependent Culture	Subject matter experts are called upon to handle work activities any hour of the day or night, often resulting in lost productivity and burnout.
Physical Review	A requirements gathering technique that involves formal tours, demonstrations, and informal visits to the various areas to be supported.

Term	Definition
Plan	A formal, approved document that describes the capabilities and resources needed to achieve a desired result.
Policy	A formal document that describes the overall intentions and direction of a service provider, as formally expressed by senior management.
Proactive culture	People use information to anticipate customer needs (i.e., "fire prevention").
Problem Management	(ISO/IEC 20000) Process that minimizes disruption to the business by proactive identification and analysis of the cause of incidents and by managing problems to closure.
Procedure	A step-by-step set of instructions that describe how to perform the tasks in a process.
Process	A collection of interrelated work activities that take a set of specific inputs and produce a set of specific outputs that are of value to a customer.
Process Definition Document (PDD)	A formal document used to record and maintain the details of all process components.
Process-Dependent Culture	Knowledge is captured and reused and roles and responsibilities are clearly defined, resulting in effective use of subject matter experts, and providing opportunities for growth.
Process Design Workbook	A document that provides a brief assessment of the current environment and a summary of all decisions made to date.
Process Design Workshop	A workshop where all stakeholders are led by a facilitator through a series of exercises aimed at designing or redesigning a process.
Process Framework	Describes best practices that can be used to define and continually improve a given set of processes.
Process Improvement Priority Matrix	A matrix used to map processes eligible for design or improvement against improvement criteria.
Process Improvement Team (PIT)	A team of individuals that designs or redesigns a process and determines how best to implement the new process across the organization.
Process Manager	The individual who is responsible for operational (day-to-day) management of a process.
Process Maps	A diagram that shows the sequence of tasks that occur within a process and also the relationship a process has with other processes. Process maps can assume several forms including: high-level integration maps, relationship maps, cross-functional maps, and flowcharts.

Term	Definition
Process Maturity	A reflection of how well a process is defined, how capable it is of being continually improved through the use of measures tied to business goals, and how well it is embedded in the organization's culture.
Process Overview	A brief narrative description of a process that includes its objectives and goals, along with information such as the process owner, the process's boundaries, triggers, inputs, suppliers, tasks/activities, outputs, customers, and metrics.
Process Owner	The individual who is accountable for overall process quality and ensures conformance to the process.
Program	A group of related projects managed in a coordinated way to obtain benefits that cannot be achieved by managing the projects individually.
Program Management	The process of managing a group of related projects in a coordinated way to achieve the program's strategic goals and benefits.
Project	A temporary endeavor undertaken to create a unique product, service, or result (Project Management Body of Knowledge, Project Management Institute).
Project Charter	A short document that formally authorizes the project and empowers the project manager.
Project Management Office (PMO)	A group or department that centralizes, coordinates, and oversees the management of projects, programs, or a combination of both.
Project Manager	The individual who leads a project team and is assigned the authority and responsibility for overseeing the project and meeting the project's objectives.
Project Plan	A set of documents that describe a project, its objectives, and how the objectives are to be achieved.
Project Scope Statement	A document that describes in detail the work to be done and serves as an agreement between all stakeholders of the project.
Project Sponsor	The individual who has ultimate authority over the project and secures project funding.
Proof of Concept	Evidence that an idea or concept is feasible.
Quality	Conformance to customer requirements.
Quality Management System (QMS)	A framework for continual quality improvement.
Quick Win	A result achieved within a short period of time with relatively little effort.

Term	Definition
RACI Matrix	A matrix used to map roles and responsibilities to the activities of a process. A RACI matrix can also be used to map the roles and responsibilities of the people and teams engaged in a project with project tasks. A RACI matrix indicates who is responsible, accountable, consulted and informed. Also known as an ARCI Matrix.
RACIVS	A variation of a RACI matrix which reflects who *verifies* that an outcome meets acceptance criteria and who *signs* off on the verified outcome.
RASCI	A variation of a RACI matrix which reflects a *support* role allocated to a responsible role.
Reactive Culture	People simply react to events that occur each day (i.e., "firefighting").
Reengineering	The fundamental rethinking and radical redesign of business processes to achieve dramatic improvements in critical, contemporary measures of performance, such as cost, quality, service, and speed.
Relationship Map	A process map that shows the supplier and customer relationships that exist within the boundaries of a process, the process activities, and the inputs and outputs produced.
Release Management	(ISO/IEC 20000) Process to deliver, distribute, and track one or more changes in a release into the live environment.
Results that Matter	Performance measurement initiatives aimed at ensuring every department within the government has the tools and data needed for all employees to focus on delivering results that matter to citizens.
Return on Investment (ROI)	A calculation that measures the quantifiable benefit derived from an investment and compares it with the total cost of the project.
Request for Information (RFI)	A form or letter that asks for specific product information relative to a company's requirements.
Request for Proposal (RFP)	A form or letter that requires financial information as well as specific product information relative to a company's requirements.
Requirement	Something that is required; a necessity.
Requirements Definition Document (RDD)	A formal document that describes the customer and stakeholder requirements for a service, process, or project, along with a recommended solution.
Risk	A possible event that could cause injury or loss or affect the ability to realize a benefit.
Role-Based Training	A training strategy that maps the skills that people need to their responsibilities and level of authority.

Term	Definition
Roles and Responsibilities	The roles required to perform a process (including customers and suppliers) and the activities or tasks performed by each role.
Run Chart	A graph used to chart process variations over time. See also control chart.
Scatter Diagram	A graph used to show how two pairs of variables are related. Also known as a scatter plot.
Service Continuity and Availability Management	(ISO/IEC 20000) Process to ensure that agreed service continuity and availability commitments to customers can be met in all circumstances.
Service Level Agreement (SLA)	A written document that spells out the services that IT will provide the customer, the agreed upon and funded level of service performance, how service performance is measured, and the customer's responsibilities.
Service Level Management (SLM)	(ISO/IEC 20000) Process to define, agree, record, and manage levels of service.
Service Level Requirement (SLR)	A customer requirement.
Service Management Program Owner	The individual responsible for the overall service management program.
Service Reporting	(ISO/IEC 20000) Process to produce agreed, timely, reliable, and accurate reports for informed decision making and effective communication.
Seven Basic Tools of Quality	Simple but powerful data analysis tools that can be used to solve the majority of quality problems. The seven basic tools of quality are: cause-and-effect diagrams (also called Ishikawa or fishbone diagrams), check sheets, control or run charts, flowcharts, histograms, Pareto charts, and scatter diagrams.
Six Sigma	A disciplined, data-driven approach and methodology for eliminating defects in any process.
Six Sigma DMADV	Steps used to develop new processes or products at Six Sigma quality levels or for incremental process improvement. DMADV steps include: Define, Measure, Analyze, Design and Verify.
Six Sigma DMAIC	Steps used to incrementally improve processes that are failing to meet performance specifications. DMAIC steps include: Define, Measure, Analyze, Improve, and Control.
Software Design Committee	A team that participates in the definition of screen layouts, menus, reports, etc. as needed to configure and customize a selected system to a process.
Software Selection Committee	A team that identifies system requirements following process design and also identifies and evaluates systems that conform to those requirements and makes a final recommendation to management.

Term	Definition
Stakeholder	Any person or group who is or might be affected by a service, process, or project.
Standard	(ISO) A document that contains an agreed-upon and approved set of requirements that an organization must satisfy to be certified.
Sub-process	A logically grouped lower-level view of activities performed within a process.
Supplier	(Process) A creator of process input.
Supplier Management	(ISO/IEC 20000) Process to manage suppliers to ensure the provision of seamless, quality services.
Supporting Processes	Processes that govern or control and support business activities (e.g., accounting, corporate governance, human resources, and IT service management).
Tangible Benefit	A benefit that is capable of being measured precisely. Tangible benefits are typically expressed in financial terms.
Task	A piece of work assigned to a single individual.
Team Ground Rules	The rules a team agrees to live by to facilitate teamwork.
Technical Specialists	Individuals who are responsible for facilitating the implementation and administration of associated technologies.
Technical Writer	An individual who assists with the creation of required documents, procedures, and training materials.
Technology	The tools and technologies people use to do their work.
Technology Selection Report	A report that describes the selection process you followed and how the final decision was made.
Ten Process Design and Improvement Steps	A methodology that can be used to design and improve any process regardless of maturity level.
To Be Flowchart	A flowchart that shows how a new process is to be performed once implemented.
Total Quality Control (TQC)	A quality management approach to continuing improvement through statistical quality control. See *kaizen*.
Total Quality Management (TQM)	A quality management approach to long-term success through customer satisfaction.
Training	Practical education (i.e., learning to do).
Tribal Knowledge	Unwritten ways of working.
Trigger	An event that initiates, or triggers, the start of a process.
Value Chain	A concept that involves categorizing the value-adding activities of an organization and beyond.
Value Network	A complex set of relationships between two or more individuals, groups, or organizations.

Term	Definition
Value Network Analysis	A technique that enables organizations to understand and optimize the relationships within a value network.
Value on Investment	A measurement of the expected benefit of an investment. It represents both the financial (tangible) and non-monetary (intangible) value created by an investment.
Weight	The weight of importance assigned to each of your requirements.
World-Class	A company that has achieved and is able to sustain high levels of customer satisfaction.
Work Instructions	A detailed set of instructions that describe how to perform a single task.

Index